Songs of the North Woods
as sung by O. J. Abbott and collected by Edith Fowke

Songs of the North Woods
as sung by O. J. Abbott and collected by Edith Fowke

László Vikár
and
Jeanette Panagapka

UNIVERSITY OF
CALGARY
PRESS

©2004 Jeanette Panagapka and László Vikár

Published by the University of Calgary Press
2500 University Drive NW Calgary, Alberta, Canada T2N 1N4
www.uofcpress.com

No part of this publication may be reproduced, stored in a retrieval system or transmitted, in any form or by any means, without the prior written consent of the publisher or a licence from The Canadian Copyright Licensing Agency (Access Copyright). For an Access Copyright licence, visit www.accesscopyright.ca or call toll free to 1-800-893-5777.

We acknowledge the financial support of the Government of Canada through the Book Publishing Industry Development Program (BPIDP), the Alberta Foundation for the Arts and the Alberta Lottery Fund—Community Initiatives Program for our publishing activities. We acknowledge the support of the Canada Council for the Arts for our publishing program.

Cover and page design, Mieka West

Library and Archives Canada Cataloguing in Publication

Songs of the North woods [music] : as sung by O. J. Abbott and collected by Edith Fowke / edited by László Vikár and Jeanette Panagapka.

ISBN 1-55238-077-7

1. Folk songs, English—Ottawa River Valley (Québec and Ont.) I. Abbott, O. J. II. Fowke, Edith, 1913- III. Panagapka, Jeanette, 1940- IV. Vikár, László.

M1678.S69834 2004   782.42162'09713'8   C2004-905288-8

Contents

VI	Foreword
VIII	Preface I
X	Preface II
XV	Acknowledgments
XVI	Introduction
1	Songs
70	Song Analysis
74	Edith Fowke
77	O. J. Abbott
80	Interview with Frank Fowke
85	Interview with Richard Johnston
89	Appendix A: Stories of O. J. Abbott
93	Books and Recordings by Edith Fowke
97	Bibliography
98	Discography
99	Index of Songs
100	Alphabetical Index
101	Index of First Lines
103	Abstract
104	Songs Sung by O. J. Abbott
108	Notes

Brouse & Brouse General Store
Rapides des Joachims
Quebec.

Foreword

Traditional music or folk music is one of the defining aspects of a culture. The texts of folk songs preserve the history and illuminate the struggles and triumphs of a people, as well as portray the more mundane aspects of the daily lives of individuals at work and play. Their words tell us the way things were perceived at specific times, and in particular places; they tell us, not only what happened, but how people felt about what happened. If these were all folk songs offered, there would be reason enough to preserve them. However, folk songs are also a treasure house of interesting poetry and beautiful melodies, many with antecedents centuries old.

Today we are in danger of losing that rich resource. Folk songs came into being orally. They were passed from one singer to another and from one generation to the next through singing. In the course of this transmission, tunes were varied and texts were altered to suit the singers and their situations. This change and variation was the lifeblood of the folk process. With the advent at the beginning of the twentieth century of recorded sound, and later of radio, television, and the web, this folk process was unalterably changed. Traditional songs were still being sung, now over the airwaves, but they were often broadcast with instrumental accompaniment, in stylistically inaccurate performances, which were then reproduced by the listening public as heard. They were as fixed as photographs. The process of alteration and variation ceased to exist.

Fortunately, it was at this point, during the early and mid-twentieth century, that scholars began to take an interest in collecting and preserving songs from those communities and people who still had a lively oral tradition. In Canada, Marius Barbeau collected songs in Québec, Helen Creighton in Nova Scotia, Kenneth Peacock in Newfoundland. And Edith Fowke ventured into the small communities of northern Ontario to collect the songs of lumberjacks.

To these pioneering collectors we owe the preservation of Canadian traditional music. Folksong researchers may refer to their recordings and written documents for study, performers could find in them a rich source of interesting material, composers might take inspiration from them, and teachers could utilize them with children.

However, many more songs were collected than were ever transcribed. It is exciting to collect songs, while it is painstaking, exacting work to turn audiotapes into written notation. Further, some collectors simply did not possess the necessary musical knowledge to do so. Edith Fowke was among the latter. While she had a consuming interest in folk song, she freely admitted that she was not a musician and did not possess the skill needed to put the songs she collected into print.

When Edith Fowke first met László Vikár in 1977 they discussed the possibility of his transcribing some of her, by that time, significant, as yet untranscribed, collection. Dr. Vikár, a member of the Hungarian Academy of Sciences Folk Music Research Group, had spent much of his life, like Edith, collecting folk songs, but had spent at least as much time notating and analyzing the songs he collected. These are published in a number of volumes. He is an internationally acknowledged authority on folk music transcription and analysis.

Work on the present volume began shortly before Edith Fowke's death in 1996. While Dr. Vikár's expertise in the musical aspects of the work brought a high level of precision and exactitude to that part of the work, it was deemed important to have someone whose native language was English to deal with the transcription of texts. Jeanette Panagapka, a native of Ontario, had studied with Edith Fowke and had worked with Dr. Vikár for many years, first as a student, and later as a colleague. She was a natural choice as co-author.

The work was greatly facilitated when Edith Fowke left her entire collection of tapes, books, and records to the University of Calgary, where she had taught folk music to teachers in graduate summer courses. Research grants from the university made it possible to transfer the old and fragile reel-to-reel tapes to a more durable form, and to bring the authors together to begin the work of transcription and analysis.

Much remains to be done with the Edith Fowke bequest, but this present volume represents a significant addition to the core of authentic Canadian folk music now in print.

Lois Choksy, DFA
Professor Emeritus of Music
University of Calgary

Preface I

László Vikár

More than forty years ago, in July 1960, during the 13th Conference of the International Folk Music Council (IFMC)[1] held in Vienna, Austria, I had the pleasure of meeting one of the first Canadian experts in folk music research. For several days I was able to enjoy the company of Marius Barbeau – already a legendary great old man – who recounted with enthusiasm his memories of decades of field research. He was the one who told of his meetings on the British Columbia shores of the Pacific Ocean with remote Native tribes. He recalled the difficulties and the beauty of recording, and later of transcribing this very special musical heritage. He was attentive not only to the dialects of these people but even more so to the musical expressions – so different from the well-known English/French music. Even in my greatest imagination I could not conceive that the time would come when I would be able to meet these First Nations Peoples.

Three years later, in the summer of 1963, in Jerusalem, Israel, I had the opportunity to meet Kenneth Peacock, who gave a lecture during the 16th Conference of the IFMC, presided over by Zoltán Kodály. Peacock's lecture gave us insight into the musical tradition of the Atlantic side of Canada – the fishing songs of Newfoundland. The result of his research was published not long after this meeting in three large volumes.

In the spring of 1971 the possibility arose for me to give lectures about the method and results of Hungarian ethnomusicology, founded by Bartók and Kodály, during a six-week course in Montréal. Here I was able to demonstrate the close and useful relationship between folk music research and music education. During these six weeks I was fortunate enough to travel twice to Nova Scotia. Both excursions were planned in order to meet with Helen Creighton, who was an outstanding authority on Maritime music which was rooted deeply in Western European musical cultures.

The following year I learned even more as I had the opportunity to visit two large archives – probably the two largest archives of folk songs in Canada – first in Québec City and then in Ottawa. To my delight and surprise I found, in Québec City, almost 40,000 detailed transcriptions of old French songs from Québec, Acadia, and even Louisiana, preserved conscientiously in those areas. Roger Matton, an outstanding composer and head of the archives, kindly guided me through this collection.

Just two weeks later, in Ottawa, I became acquainted with the very large and carefully organized collection of English-language folk songs in the National Museum of Canada [Museum of Civilization].

Thus in such a short time I learned much about the characteristics of the folk music of this enormous bilingual country.

It was at the 1978 Congress of the International Society of Music Education (ISME) in London, Ontario, that I was honoured to meet Edith Fowke, whose substantial knowledge of folk music was recognized throughout Canada. During our discussions she expressed an interest in the possibility of an unusual cooperation between us. At that time she must have heard about the Kodály concept, an approach to music education based on the musical mother-tongue – folk songs. In short, she told me, it could be useful for us to have a Canadian folk song collection that would focus on the music as well as the lyrics.

Edith expressed an opinion that this would throw more light on the partnership between music and language. Not only the text, but also the melodies should be understood and transmitted to the next generation. Now, twenty years later, I have returned to this idea. Edith Fowke's suggestion, and my almost thirty years of teaching summer courses in Canada – in Québec, Ontario, Alberta – gave me the impetus to think about the realization of this project. During this time several hundred teachers studying with me recognized with great pleasure the usefulness of our practice. Any time I met the late professor Richard Johnston, he always encouraged me to share our experiences with Canadians.

Recently I learned that the whole collection of field recordings made by Edith Fowke was donated to the University of Calgary. This, and a Visiting Scholar Grant at that university set the wheels in motion to listen to, and to transcribe a segment of this invaluable material.

To be realistic, I had to focus on a particular part – namely the songs of one good singer – the songs of O. J. Abbott. The project has been undertaken in collaboration with Jeanette Panagapka, who transcribed the texts of the songs, conducted the interviews and researched the information about Edith Fowke. A number of O. J. Abbott's songs have been published previously in collections. However, there has been little attempt at musical analysis and comparison in any of these collections. This present publication could be useful because it compares the same, the similar, and the different musical motifs and structures. It could be used first of all in Canada, but threads of the music go back to the England and the Celtic Nations, especially Ireland.

No doubt, there are advantages and disadvantages in having someone from abroad undertaking such a publication. The most obvious disadvantage is that the author might not have been as much in touch with local traditions as someone who was born here. On the other hand it could be that someone from outside may look with fresh eyes, and no preconceptions. He may set this tradition in a larger context.

Finally, I must thank all Canadians, whether I have met them or not, who contributed to this song collection. To the singer, O. J. Abbott, who passed away long ago, and to my colleagues, and friends who helped me, I express my appreciation.

Calgary, July 1999.

Preface II

Jeanette Panagapka

Songs of the North Woods is truly an international collaboration. The manuscript has travelled between Canada and Hungary numerous times. Dr. László Vikár transcribed the music and I, Jeanette Panagapka, transcribed the texts. Together we fitted text to music, proofread, and edited.

Dr. Vikár is a noted ethnomusicologist, Professor of Ethnomusicology at the Liszt Academy of Music in Budapest, Hungary, and former head of the Folkmusic Division of the Institute of Musicology, Hungarian Academy of Sciences. He is one of the few persons still alive who worked extensively with Zoltán Kodály in the Folk Music Group of the Academy of Sciences before the composer's death in 1967. Dr. Vikár's personal collection of songs from Hungary and the Kama-Volga area of Russia numbers over eight thousand and has resulted in numerous books and articles. For many years Dr. Vikár taught in the Kodály Summer Program at the University of Calgary. He considers this publication to be his contribution to the preservation of Canadian traditional music.

My interest in traditional music stems from a career in music education utilizing the Kodály method. Singing and literacy are the focus of Kodály-based music programs and traditional songs are the principal musical material used. There is a need in such programs for a large repertoire of traditional songs and an understanding of their musical elements. For many years I taught courses on the Kodály approach to music education at Wilfrid Laurier University in Waterloo, Ontario, and at the University of Calgary in Alberta.

Because of the specific focus each of us brought to this volume, we have both written prefaces. In his preface Dr. Vikár elaborates on the musical transcriptions and the nature of transcribing. I discuss the historical and anecdotal aspects of the book.

In discussions with Edith Fowke we decided to concentrate on the songs of just one singer. She suggested O. J. Abbott as he was certainly one of her favourite singers. It was also her wish that the emphasis in this book be on the music and musical analysis. In a letter to Lois Choksy, dated November 23, 1996, Edith says of O. J. Abbott, "Next to La Rena Clark, he had the largest repertoire of any of my singers, and many of the best songs."[2] His songs are primarily descended from older Irish tunes and they cover a wide range of topics such as love, war, humour, and lumbering. Many are ballads with multiple verses.

In undertaking the research for this book we had hoped to find field notes with detailed information about the songs. Unfortunately there is no dialogue on Edith Fowke's field recordings other than the two stories included in the book. She left her books, papers, field recordings, and vinyl recordings to Special Collections, University of Calgary Library, and the copyright to all published and unpublished works to the Writers' Union of Canada. In this collection there are no field notes related to the songs of O. J. Abbott, leading us to believe that none exist. Edith Fowke had a phenomenal memory, and it would seem that much of the information about the songs was stored in her head. The only information we could locate about the songs comes from notes in previous publications and commercial recordings by Edith Fowke that contain songs by O. J. Abbott. The obituary for O. J. Abbott in the Ottawa Citizen, March 5, 1962, states that a collection of tapes of his songs is stored in the National Museum in Ottawa. The Museum of Civilization kindly provided a list of the thirty-two songs in their collection and it is included in the Appendix.

Much of the information about O. J. Abbott and about Edith Fowke has come from presentation papers, lecture notes, and articles in the University of Calgary archives. Some of these are titled and dated. Many of them are not. Much of the information is repetitious from one text to another. However, they have proven to be a valuable resource in the preparation of Songs of the North Woods.

The recording of the songs of O. J. Abbott, Irish and British Songs from the Ottawa Valley Sung by O. J. Abbott (Folkways FM 4051) contains extensive liner notes and the texts of all twenty-three songs on the recording. It is curious that this recording was not followed up with a book of the musical transcriptions of the songs. There are two possible reasons for this. In several of her papers, Edith expresses a strong belief that people should hear the original singers and learn the songs by oral transmission. This is reflected in the number of recordings that she produced, the CBC program Folk Song Time, and the occasions at which she had the singers, including O. J. Abbott, perform. Perhaps a more practical reason was that transcription was not something Edith could do herself as she was not a trained musician.

In our study of the O. J. Abbott tapes we observed that he had a distinctive singing style and speech patterns that were typical of the Ottawa valley. Many of the songs begin with "Oh," which he would hold for a considerable time. At the climax of the song, usually on a high note, he would pause again. The last word was always spoken. Sometimes it would take until the second verse for him to be really clear about the tune. This is not uncommon when one is singing many songs, changing from one key to another, and shifting to a different tempo or another mood.

O. J. Abbott sang approximately 120 songs for Edith Fowke. Many of these have multiple verses while some are simply fragments. From these, we chose sixty-six songs we considered to be the most musically interesting. It is always a challenge to make a selection, but Edith Fowke, in her introduction to A Family Heritage: The Story and Songs of LaRena Clark, says "we narrowed our selection by concentrating on those that were unique or rare, were particularly complete or well worded, or showed some interesting textual or musical variations."[3] In the previously mentioned letter to Lois Choksy (November 23, 1996) Edith suggested that "a total of sixty to seventy songs would be desirable." Twenty-six of the sixty-six O. J. Abbott songs we chose have been previously published, however, we transcribed all of the songs in Songs of the North Woods from the original tapes without reference to earlier printed versions.

Canada lost a national treasure in March of 1996 when Edith Fowke died. In the 1950s, when it was barely acceptable for women to work, Edith was out collecting stories and songs from the common folk of Ontario. In succeeding years she published numerous articles and some thirty books on both folklore and folk music.

Although she was not a trained musician, Edith made a significant contribution to folklore, to the study and performance of traditional music, and to music education. I doubt that there is anyone teaching music or performing traditional songs who has not used songs from Folksongs of Canada, Sally Go Round the Sun, The Penguin Book of Canadian Folksongs, Singing Our History, or Canada's Story in Song. We have included a listing of the books and recordings by Edith Fowke that may be found in Special Collections, University of Calgary Library.

Shortly before her death, I had occasion to visit Edith several times. She was keenly interested in the conception of this book and gave us valuable guidance. After her death, I interviewed both her husband, Frank Fowke, and Richard Johnston, her co-author for Folksongs of Canada. These interviews were transcribed and are included. They are of interest historically and musically. In addition, we transcribed two stories as told to Edith Fowke by O. J. Abbott.

Both Richard Johnston and Frank Fowke attest to the fact that Edith was a very independent, feisty lady. As a co-author of Folksongs of Canada, Johnston said that they needed each other. Edith Fowke lacked training in music notation and arranging. She needed Johnston to edit the music and to write the accompaniments. He said that he did not transcribe any of the music, as many of these songs were available from other sources. All songs that were actually from Edith's own collection had been transcribed by various other people. Although Richard Johnston and Edith Fowke became friends in later years, the relationship was rather stormy at the beginning. Both of them were noted for having strong personalities and convictions.

Frank Fowke lived in Toronto until his death on June 1, 2003 in his 100th year. Before his death the transcription of his interview was read to him and it was reported to me that he had quite a chuckle hearing some of the stories again. He was a grand raconteur and was happy to share memories about Edith. He recalled that he met Edith in the mid-1930s at a dance at the University of Saskatchewan, where they were both students, Edith in English, and Frank in engineering.

I asked Frank how Edith became interested in folk music. He recounted that they had an early record player and began collecting recordings, mostly of folk songs. When Edith found herself out of a job shortly after the war, she persuaded Harry Boyle at the Canadian Broadcasting Corporation (CBC) to let her present a program on folk music using her recordings. This evolved into Folk Song Time, which was on the air for a number of years. One summer in the early 1950s, she and Frank took a holiday in Nova Scotia and decided to look up Helen Creighton, the noted collector of Nova Scotia folksongs. They found her along the coast in Nova Scotia collecting folk music with a tape recorder. This was one of the first times Edith had seen a tape recorder used for such a purpose, and she became quite interested in the possibility of collecting songs herself in this way. The first tape recorder that Edith used was so heavy that she could not lift it so Frank went with her in the early years. In my interview with him he recounted several stories about those trips — stories that have been included.

Edith Fowke donated her collection of 150 field recordings (representing some two thousand songs), 1,000 books, and numerous papers to Special Collections, University of Calgary Library. However, in her will, Edith left the copyright to this collection to the Writers' Union of Canada. This valuable material is now available (with permission from TWUC) to anyone involved in the study or performance of traditional music. Edith's interest in leaving her life's work to the University of Calgary began when she taught in the Kodály Summer Diploma Program in the early 1980s. Classes were delighted by this diminutive, white-haired lady always dressed in pink. The lady-like, fragile Edith Fowke the students saw was hard to reconcile with the image of the pioneering Edith Fowke who had been collecting folksongs in the field on reel-to-reel tape from lumbermen in backwoods logging camps.

In the months before Edith died, I met with her on several occasions to arrange for the transport of her reel-to-reel tapes from Toronto to Calgary. Because of the fragile nature of the reels, as well as their historical value, we decided that I should take back as many as I could each time I flew from Toronto to Calgary. This gave me repeated opportunities to chat with Edith about the research possibilities inherent in the collection. Edith regretted that she was not a trained musician and had never been able to transcribe the songs she collected but had to rely on others for this exacting work. Many of the songs she collected had never been transcribed and those that had been were not always musically accurate. Few were subjected to any kind of musical analysis. Edith was interested in having more thorough transcriptions and analyses undertaken and expressed particular interest in having me work, along with László Vikár, on the songs of one of her most prolific informants, O. J. Abbott. To the end, she was a delightful lady to visit. Although her body was failing, her mind, memory, and wit were razor sharp.

One of my tasks in the summer of 1996, after Edith Fowke's death, was to arrange for an inventory of the books in Edith Fowke's personal library before they could be moved to Calgary. The collection covered an entire wall of a room from floor to ceiling. Skye Morrison, Allison Lupton, and I spent a tiring, but delightful day listing the books by title. This was a mere listing, not a cataloguing. The biggest challenge was to keep from opening the cover of each book. Many of these books were rare collections of folksongs or folk tales. There were numerous articles and complete sets of journals dating back to the 1950s. We could have spent weeks happily browsing. Fortunately, Edith Fowke's collection is now available in the University of Calgary's Special Collections for anyone who is interested.

The graduate program at the University of Calgary has had a number of students (Sharyn Favreau, Luisa Izzo, Allison Lupton, Susan Drayson, and Maureen Chafe) whose research has been in the area of traditional music. This new acquisition from Edith Fowke will provide research possibilities for years to come. Sheri Herget recently completed a master's thesis on one aspect of the Edith Fowke collection of field tapes at the MacKimmie Library – Towards an Understanding of Canadian Traditional Song Style through Analyses of Descriptive Transcriptions using Field Recordings Made by Edith Fowke in the Peterborough Area of Ontario during the Years 1957 to 1959 (Master's thesis, University of Calgary, 2001).

Edith Fowke's interest in preserving our Canadian cultural heritage through the collection and dissemination of folk music and folklore is perpetuated through her gift to the University of Calgary, through the many people whose lives she touched, and through publications such as this.

Gibsons, B.C., April 2004

Acknowledgments

The authors would like to acknowledge the following assistance in the preparation of Songs of the North Woods:

- Edith Fowke for her diligence and foresight in collecting more than two thousand folksongs in the 1950s. Before her death in 1996 we had the opportunity to discuss the concept of this book with her on several occasions. We are grateful for her interest and input in Songs of the North Woods, as well as for her permission to transcribe the songs of O. J. Abbott.
- The Writers' Union of Canada for permission to publish the songs, stories and interviews collected by Edith Fowke as well as quotes from unpublished letters and documents.
- The University of Calgary for two research grants. The first, a University of Calgary Research Grant, allowed for the reel-to-reel tapes to be transferred to cassette format. The second, a Visiting Scholar Grant, provided funds for Dr. Vikár to come to Calgary in January 1997 to begin the work of transcription and analysis.
- The Canadian Society for Traditional Music for permission to use the unpublished papers of Edith Fowke for research.
- The Canadian Museum of Civilization in Ottawa for permission to list the songs of O. J. Abbott that are in their collection.
- Frank Fowke for permission to print the interview with him, as well as a photo of Edith Fowke, and encouragement in the writing of this book.
- Bernard Abbott for permission to print excerpts from my interview with him, as well as photos of his father, O. J. Abbott.
- Eugene Cramer, executor of the estate of Richard Johnston, for permission to print the interview with Richard Johnston.
- Apollonia Steele of the Special Collections Branch for her encouragement and research assistance.
- Lois Choksy for essential support, valued critical comment, and editing of the manuscript.
- Maureen Chafe and John Abram who assisted with initial computer notation of songs, and Shane Fage for some initial transcriptions.
- Karen Taylor and Eugene Cramer for reading and commenting on the manuscript.
- To all who supported and contributed to the publication of this book, particularly Dr. Eugene Cramer

Introduction

Two approaches to the transcription of melodies are used by ethnomusicologists. The most common practice involves a simple transcription usually containing only half, quarter, and eighth notes, and rests, and staying within the framework of 2/4, 3/4, 4/4, or 6/8 metres. In most collections, even at an international level, one may find this kind of notation of the melodies. Songs notated in this way can be sung easily by individuals or groups. They are musically appropriate for school use or for beginning literacy programs. However, this kind of transcription gives only the skeleton of the real music.

A more scientific method involves a detailed transcription that tries to demonstrate even the tiniest parts of the melody and the rhythm of the original performance. In this picture there may be several grace notes or passing notes, intervals of less than a minor second, and a great number of irrational rhythmic patterns, such as septola, or 7/8. This latter approach to transcription is used primarily by experts who need such details for comparative analyses. This process is similar to putting objects under the microscope in order to know more about them. The detailed transcriptions may approach reality, however, the limits of the human senses cannot comprehend the whole. The perfect picture can be reached only through technology for which the possibility already exists. However, computer notation, while exact, is frequently both unreadable and unmusical, and is not yet used much in actual practice.

The melodies themselves often dictate the best method of transcription. There is no way to write down a simple melody in a complicated form. On the other hand, it would make no sense to transcribe a free-rhythm song in a simple way because the essence of this kind of music would be completely lost. Between the extremities of the simplest and the most complicated transcriptions there are endless other solutions. The final notation of the melody is determined by the person who is transcribing, and by the purpose of the work. In some instances both the simple and the detailed transcriptions are published.

It may be helpful to say a few words about the form in which songs appear in this publication. The simplest, and the best notation is, of course, one phrase on one line. The reader may, in this way, immediately recognize the musical form. It would be confusing to publish four phrases in three or five lines just because of space or technical problems, and yet this occurs in numerous song collections.

When publishing folk songs, it is not necessary to keep the original tonality. Most singers do not repeat a song in the same key another time. The internationally accepted g finalis is used for scientific research, but it forces the reader/singer into a range that is often unsingable because the octave is too high. For practical reasons the range is best between low a and the high e, a range in which most people sing easily. The last note of the song should accommodate this range, and at the same time avoid too many key signatures. Songs in this collection have therefore been notated to facilitate easy singing. An appropriate metronome indication preserves the original character of each melody. The use of words to indicate the tempo could be misinterpreted, e.g., "Moderato" could range between 72 and 104. In some detailed transcriptions there may be different tempi within a song, but never in a simple one, except in some refrains.

It may happen that the informant is insecure in some places when singing. However, it would be a mistake to write this into a simple transcription. The body position (sitting or standing), lack of memory, age, or general health may affect the pitch, or even more, the rhythm. Logic and knowledge of musical orthography can easily correct these insufficiencies.

Folk song is a living entity as long as it has variants, but, of course, the variants should fit within the style of the song. If a melody is performed every time, anywhere, and by everybody in the same way, it becomes stagnant. One must strive to collect as many melodic variants as possible, and publish them together for comparative purposes. The rhythmic variations will happen naturally with the correct pronunciation of the words and with the flow of the language.

When publishing folk songs, in addition to the notes about the text, it is indispensable to use some musical indexes to show the analyses of the scale, the metre and the range. These characteristics all contribute to a better understanding of the music. In this collection the form has not been identified, as it tends to be a subjective decision. What may appear to be AAvBAv to one person may be seen by another as ABCB. However, because the songs are published by phrase, it is easy to see similarities and differences in the musical phrases.

Songs have been arranged basically from simple to complex melodies as determined by range, scale and meter. All of Edith Fowke's other published collections were arranged by textual subject. It was her wish that this publication be arranged in a musical order. Numbers 45 to 53 are in 6/8 metre but have longer text lines with more syllables. It would have been equally correct to publish them in an eight-phrase form. For the sake of consistency, we have chosen to publish them in four phrases. The beginning solfa syllable is printed above the first note of each song. This may assist in easier reading. A song in ionian or major ends on do, aeolian or minor ends on la, dorian on re and mixolydian on so. These are the only modes contained in this collection, although there are also a number of pentatonic and hexachordal songs as well.

Tonesets and scales:

- do pentatonic: do, re, mi, so, la: M2, M3, P5, M6
- la pentatonic: la, do, re, mi so: m3, P4, P5, m7
- major hexachord: do, re, mi, fa, so, la, or so, la, ti, do, re, mi; M2, M3, P4, P5, M6: 6 notes with do finalis

- major scale: do, re, mi, fa, so, la, ti: M2, M3, P4, P5, M6, M7
- minor hexachord: la, ti, do, re, mi, fa; M2, m3, P4, P5, m6: 6 notes with la finalis
- aeolian/minor is a natural minor scale, la, ti, do, re, mi, fa, so; M2, m3, P4, P5, m6, m7 with la as the finalis.
- dorian is a scale of minor character, re, mi, fa, so, la, ti, do with re as the finalis. M2, m3, P4, P5, M6, m7 An alternate solmization is la, ti, do, re, me, fi, so
- mixolydian is a scale of major character, so, la, ti, do re, mi, fa, with so as the finalis. M2, M3, P4, P5, M6, m7 An alternate solmization is do, re, mi, fa, so, la, ta.

The range is indicated below and above the finalis. Roman numerals are indicated for pitches below the finalis and arabic numerals above. Hence V – 5 (see No. 9 or 29) would indicate a range of an octave from the dominant below to the dominant above the finalis, or, in solfa, from so_1 to so. The traditional g finalis has not been used for reasons of keeping the range singable. However, if we consider the last note (finalis) of each song as 1, it is logical that the minor third is indicated as b3 and likewise the minor tenth as b10 and the major seventh as #7.

There has been no attempt to denote singing style in this collection. Although there are certain conventions, the performer must determine how he/she will present the song. This contributes to the continued well-being of traditional music. It is customary to have extended pauses of indeterminate length at the beginning and in the middle of the song. At the beginning, the singer often holds the first note to give additional singers time to join in before the song really gets started. Twenty-two of these songs begin with "Oh," which would almost certainly be held. In the middle, the pause is frequently at a climax on a high pitch for emphasis.

The music of the first verse is notated to fit the text of this verse. In subsequent verses the performer must decide how the notation will change to fit the text. The determining factor is that the stress of the syllables of the text must fit the stress of the music. In order to accomplish this, some syllables sung on one note may be sung over two notes, and visa versa. The usual realization of this would be to change a quarter note to two eighth notes, and so on.

Key signatures are indicated only where necessary. For example, a song with a do finalis on G does not require an F# in the key signature if there is no F# in the song (see numbers 7, 8, 28)

Many songs (26) are in 6/8 metre with ♩ ♪ or ♪ ♪ ♪ rhythmic motifs. Almost all of the songs begin with an anacrusis or upbeat. In both cases, this fits the lilt of the English language.

As stated in the Preface, it does not appear that Edith Fowke left any field notes, and there is no dialogue about the songs on the field recordings. Where information is available from other printed or sound sources it has been included in the complete list of songs by O. J. Abbott (Appendix B). Otherwise, there has been no attempt to trace the songs back to their source in Irish or Scottish tradition, nor has there been any attempt to follow up on the historical references in the texts.

It is to be hoped that the following songs will provide new repertoire for performing, teaching, and research.

The Songs

The Sailor's Bride

2. It's scarce six months since we were wed.
Alas how swift those moments fled,
And now we must part by the dawn of the day,
And the proud ship bears my love away.

3. The storm came on before its time.
The snow fell hissing in the brine,
And the sailor lad, so brave and true
Was carried away in the waters blue.

4. Willie, I wish I was with you,
Beneath the waves of the ocean blue,
My soul to God, my body in the sea,
And the dark blue waves rolling over me.
*My soul to God, my body in the sea,
And the mermaids weeping over me.

Repeat melody of lines 3 and 4

The Bold and Undaunted Youth

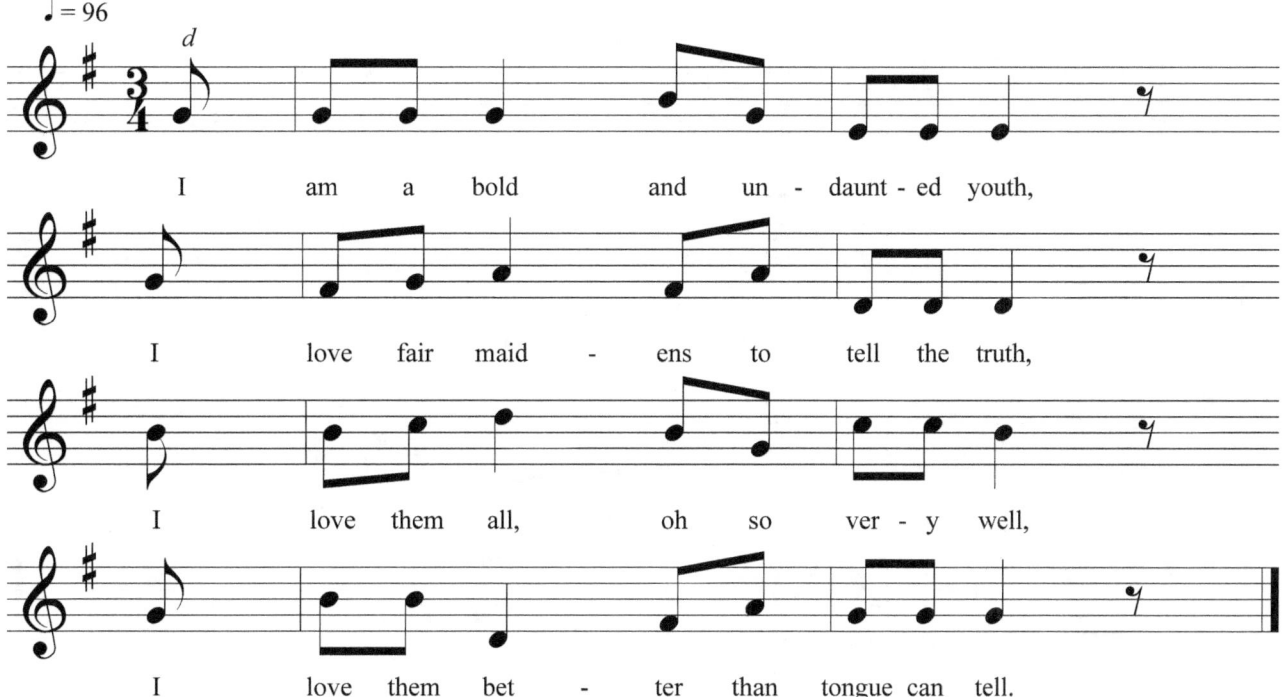

I am a bold and un-daunt-ed youth,
I love fair maid-ens to tell the truth,
I love them all, oh so ver-y well,
I love them bet-ter than tongue can tell.

2. In Stephen's Green, oh, where I was born.
In Stephen's Green where I died in scorn.
I served my time to a saddler's trade
And was a wild and a roving blade.

3. At seventeen I married a wife,
I loved her better than I loved my life,
And to maintain her, a lady gay,
I started robbing on the highway.

4. I robbed Lord Gordon, I do declare,
And Lady Elgin of Gulborn Square.
I locked the chest and bid them good-night.
I took their gold to my hearts delight.

5. In Stephen's Green, oh, where I did stray,
With my fair lady to see the play.
I'd scarce been there an hour or two
When I was taken by Lord Gordon's crew.

6. My mother cried, "Oh, my darling son."
My father cried, "Oh, he is undone."
My darling lady she tore her hair
Just like a woman in deep despair.

7. When I am dead and gone to my grave
A decent funeral pray let me have.
Six highway robbers to bury me,
Give them broadswords and their liberty.

8. Six Dublin ladies to bear my pall,
Give them white gloves and pink ribbons all.
When I am buried you may tell the truth,
I was a wild and a roving youth.

Tread on the Tail of Me Coat

Oh sure I learned my read-ing and writ-ing,
At Kil-lar-ney where I went to school.
It was there I first learned fight-ing,
With the school-mas-ter Mis-ter O'-Toole

2. He and I had many a scrimmage,
But the devil a copy I wrote.
No there wasn't a lad in the village
Dared tread on the tail of me coat.

3. I was always a devil for courting
For lessons I took in the art,
'Til cupid, the blaggert, while sporting
Drove an arrow right smack through my heart.

4. Judy O'Conner she live right for next us.
Oh, oft tender lines to her wrote,
And the blaggert who'd say a word against her
I'd tread on the tail of his coat.

5. One bog trotter, Mickey Maloney
He tried for to take her away.
He had money and I hadn't any,
So a challenge I sent him one day.

6. Next morning we met at Kilnockham,
The Shannon we crossed in a boat,
Sure I leathered him with my shillelagh,
For he trod on the tail of me coat.

7. My fame it soon spread o'er the nation,
And folks flocked to gaze upon me.
They all cried without hesitation,
"You're the fighting man, Mickey McGee."

8. Sure I beat all the Finnigan faction,
I whipped all the Murphys afloat,
And I challenged the Knowlans and Bradys
To tread on the tail of me coat.

9. To tread on the tail of me coat, ha, ha,
To tread on the tail of me coat.
Sure you might as well tread on a lion,
As tread on the tail of me coat.

Erin Go Bragh

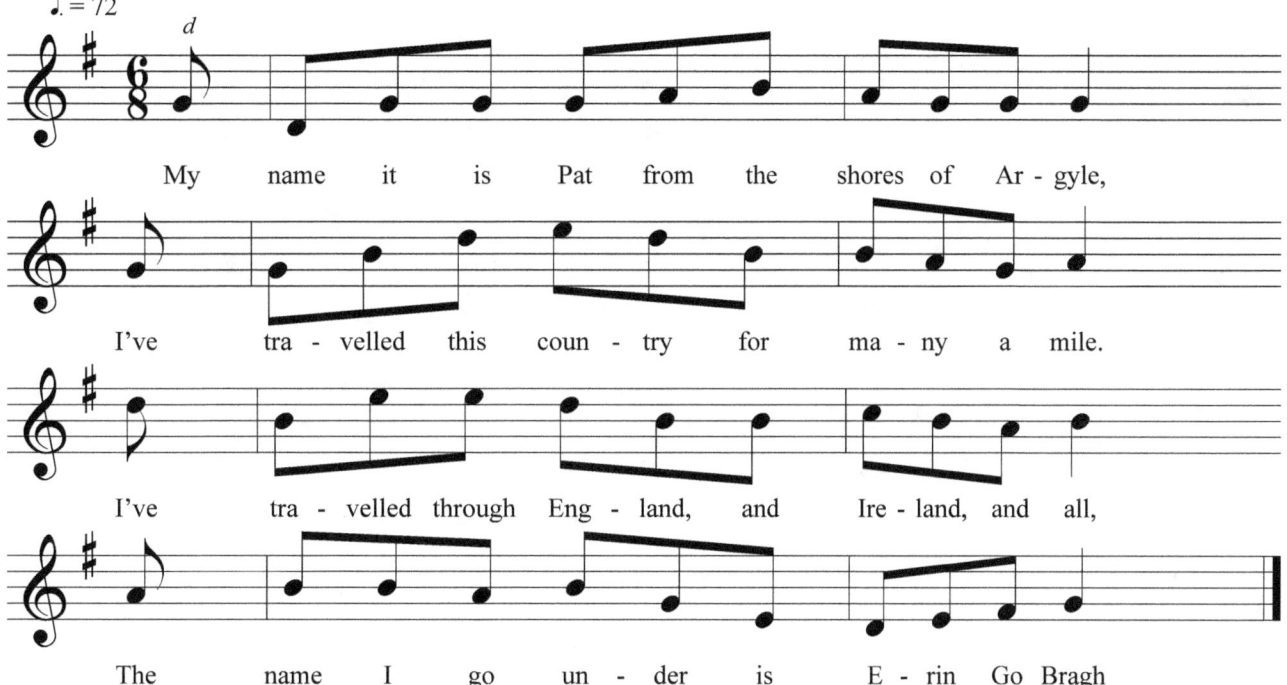

2. As I went a-walking up London main street,
A saucy policeman I chanced for to meet.
He turned up his jib and he gave me some jaw,
Saying, "Whence came you over from Erin Go Bragh?"

3. "I know you're a Paddy by the cut of your hair,
I know you're a Paddy by the clothes that you wear.
You've been banished away for breaking the law,
We see all stragglers from Erin Go Bragh."

4. "I know I'm a Paddy by the cut of my hair,
I know I'm a Paddy by the clothes that I wear.
But if I'm a Paddy that's nothing at all,
There's many a good Paddy in Erin Go Bragh."

5. A lump of a black thorn I held in me fist,
And round his big body I gave it a twist.
The blood from his head, I freely did draw,
And I showed him a trick played in Erin Go Bragh.

6. The crowd gathered round me like flocks of wild geese,
Saying, "Catch that wild Paddy, he's killed our police."
For the one friend that I had, I'm sure he had twa,
'Twas pretty hard times on old Erin Go Bragh.

7. I kicked up my heels and I steered for the north,
I jumped on a small boat that lay at the wharf.
I kick up my heels and I shouted, "Hurrah,"
Here's luck to old Ireland and Erin Go Bragh.

Johnny Gallagher

As I roved out on one morning in May,
I met Sargent Kelly by chance on my way.
He says, "Johnny Gallagher, if you'll come with me
To the fair town of Longford, strange faces you'll see."

2. I can go where I like, I've got no one to mourn,
My mother is dead and left me all alone.
My father's twice married and brought a wife home.
To me she proves cruel and does me disown.

3. We went into Jim Cairns for to have a wee dram,
And he says, "Johnny Gallagher you're a handsome young man.
You'll join the army in hopes not to rue."
He put his hand in his pocket and a shilling he drew.

4. In the taking of that shilling a bargain was made.
The ribbons were bought and I wore a cockade.
You'll go to Longford and there you will stand
To salute your noble colonel with your hat in your hand.

5. Mac and Pat Riley being a little too low,
It's straight back to Norwood they had for to go.
While I by myself was left here all alone,
Neither friend nor companion so far from my home.

6. God bless the poor mother that rears a bad son.
She doesn't know the dangers that he has to run.
All night in a guard room he will be locked in,
Neither sheet, quilt nor blanket to roll himself in.

7. My curse on my uncle where'er he may be.
If he had been an honest man and proved true to me.
If he had been an honest man and gave me a trade,
I might ne'er have joined the army nor have worn a cockade.

Chapeau Boys

I'm a jolly good fellow Pat Gregg is my name,
I came from the Chapeau that village of fame.
For singing and dancing and all other fun,
The boys from the Chapeau cannot be outdone.

2. On your patience I beg to intrude,
We lived with Fitzgerald who was agent for Booth.
To go up Black River so far, far away,
To the old Caldwell farm for to cut the hay.

3. Joe Humphrey, Bob Orme, Ned Murphy and I,
We packed up our duds on the eleventh of July.
Away up to Pembroke our luggage did take,
We boarded the Empress and sailed up the lake.

4. When we came to Fort William that place you all know,
We tuned up our fiddle and rosined our bow.
Our silver strings rang out with a clear, merry noise,
And Oiseau Rock echoes, "Well done, Chapeau Boys."

5. We headed for the Swishaw and got there all right,
We had sixteen miles to walk up to Reddy's that night.
Where we were made welcome, the truth for to speak,
It was our desire to stay there a week.

6. But we left the next morning with good wishes and smiles,
And the route to the Caldwell was forty-six miles.
North, over the mountains, Bob showed us the route,
And when we got there we were nearly played out.

7. Now the board at the Caldwell, the truth for to tell,
Could not be surpassed in the Russell Hotel.
We'd good beef and fresh mutton, our tea sweet and strong,
And great early roses full six inches long.

8. We had custard, rice pudding and sweet apple pies,
Good bread and fresh butter that would you surprise.
We had cabbage, cucumbers, boiled pickle and raw,
And the leg of a beaver we stole from a squaw.

9. Haying, being over, we packed up our dudes,
Shouldered our turkeys and off to the woods.
To fall the tall pine with our axes and saws,
To terrify the animals, the Indians and squaws.

10. I hope we'll have luck and on that we'll rely,
I hope the drive will be out by the eleventh of July.
And if we're all spared to get down in the Spring,
We'll make that old hall at the Chapeau to ring.

11. I think I'll conclude and finish my song,
I hope you won't mind me for keeping you so long.
But our cook's getting sleepy, he's nodding his head,
So we'll all say our prayers and we'll roll into bed.

The False Young Man

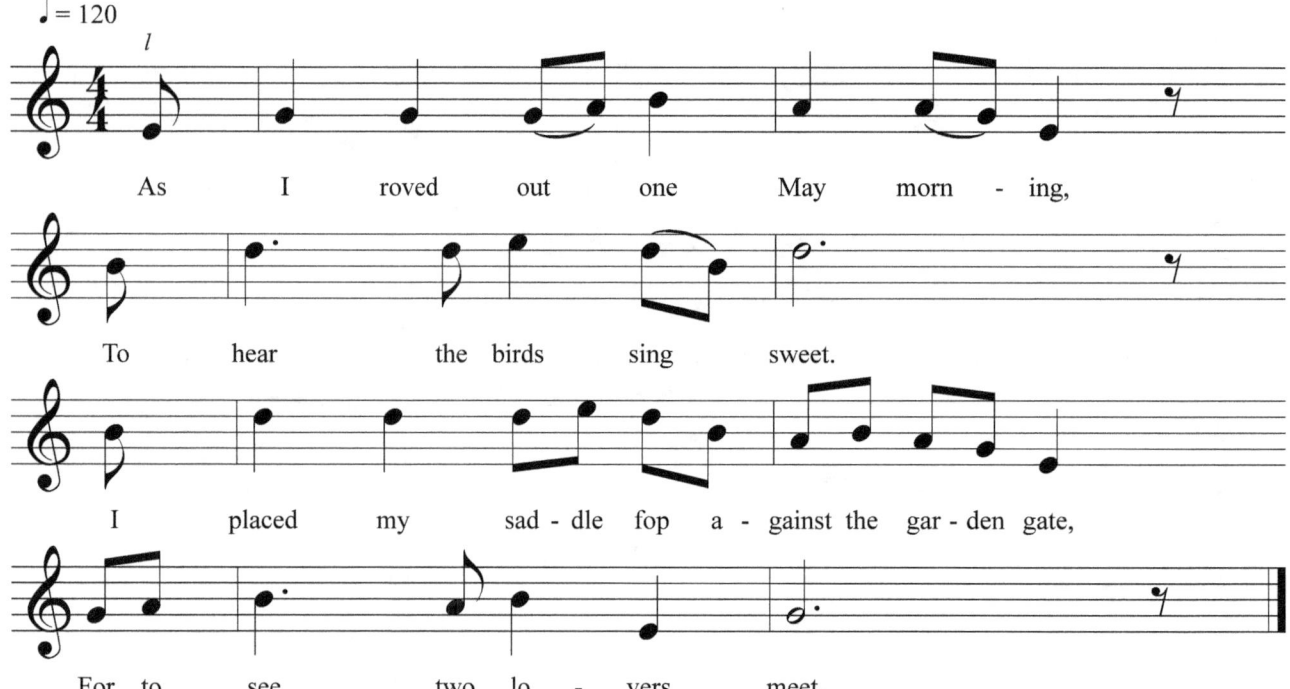

As I roved out one May morning,
To hear the birds sing sweet.
I placed my saddle fop against the garden gate,
For to see two lovers meet.

2. To see two lovers meet, my dear,
And to hear what they might say.
I would like for to know some pretty boy's mind,
Before I go away.

3. Oh, come sit down by the side of me now,
And sing a lively tune.
For it has been three quarters of a year or more,
Since together you and I have been.

4. I won't sit down by the side of you now,
No, nor any other time.
For you placed your affection on some other young girl,
And your heart is no more mine.

5. When your heart was mine, my dear,
My head lay on your breast.
And you thought I'd believe by your flattering tongue,
That the sun arose in the west.

6. There's roses in the garden for you, my dear,
There's roses in the garden for you.
But when fishes, they do fly like swallows in the sky,
Young men will then prove true.

7. You cannot mind what the old men say,
For there is some life is wrong.
Nor neither can you mind what the young men say,
For they court more girls than one.

Near the Shannon Side

Near the Shannon side there dwelt a lass, a maid both chaste and pure.
Content, she led a humble life, her circumstance being poor.
Her beauty and accomplishments did many a heart ensnare,
Oh, and many a man of high degree strove hard her love to share.

2. 'Til at length there came a-courting a farmer's only son.
By his manly resolutions her steadfast heart he won.
His manly resolutions caused her lovely eye to shine,
And in unity they did agree in wedding bans to join.

3. Some day before the wedding she says unto her dear,
"The day when we will be made one is quickly drawing near.
I must cross the Shannon side, my cousins for to see,
And there's one request I'd ask of you is to come along with me."

4. So he did agree to go with her, they went down to the shore,
And in a cot they did embark to cross the Shannon o'er.
The day being calm, the water's smooth, as side by side they sat,
And, as lover's do they did indulge in some amusing chat.

5. But when they reached the other side, the winds began to blow,
'Twas then their small and slender craft was driven to and fro.
Wave after wave came pouring in, which filled their hearts with grief,
And they called aloud to God on high to send them some relief.

6. "Oh, Rachel dear, we need not fear, we're born but for to die,
And yet it's hard, in reach of land, that here we both must lie."
He took her in his arms and he kissed her o'er and o'er,
Saying, "Farewell, oh, Rachel dear, since time it is no more."

7. Then being in a worried state, he quickly reached the land,
And turning round to view her fate, he saw her outstretched hand.
His coat, his hat, his vest, his boots, he quickly from him drew,
Saying, "Rachel dear, I'll never yield, I'll die along with you."

8. He quickly reached her sinking form, and caught her by the hand.
By force of strength, and courage too, he brought her safe to land.
The birds on each convenient bush, they sang a melody,
As if they meant for to resolve this act of loyalty.

A Young Man Lived in Belfast Town

A young man lived in Belfast town, courted a girl when she was young,
A young man lived in Belfast town, courted a girl when she was young,
He asked her for a favour bright, if he might sleep with her all night,
Right whack-fa-la diddle-i-doe-day, Right whack-fa-la diddle-i-doe-day.

2. This fair maid she gave consent, straight up to her room she went,
This fair maid she gave consent, straight up to her room she went,
And in that room there was a chair, and under the chair was crockery ware.
Right whack-fa-la did-dle-i-doe-day, Right whack-fa-la did-dle-i-doe-day.

3. This young man got up in the night, looking for his heart's delight,
This young man got up in the night, looking for his heart's delight,
His foot did slip I do declare, and he tumbled into the crockery ware.
Right whack-fa-la did-dle-i-doe-day, Right whack-fa-la did-dle-i-doe-day.

4. The old woman she got such a fright, run upstairs with the candlelight,
The old woman she got such a fright, run upstairs with the candlelight,
She says, "Young man, what brings you here, breaking all my crockery ware?"
Right whack-fa-la did-dle-i-doe-day, Right whack-fa-la did-dle-i-doe-day.

5. The police were sent for at break of day to see what this young man should pay,
The police were sent for at break of day to see what this young man should pay,
He paid nine pound for the crockery ware, and nine pound ten for the damned old chair.
Right whack-fa-la did-dle-i-doe-day, Right whack-fa-la did-dle-i-doe-day.

The Lovely Banks of Boyne

I'm a brok-en-heart-ed dam-sel, I loved a lad-die well,
My heart was al-ways true to him and it's more than tongue can tell.
'Twas at my fath-er's cas-tle he first gained that heart of mine,
And he tempt-ed me to wan-der on the love-ly banks of Boyne.

2. Oh, at first he gained my heart, then he promised that we'd wed.
But when my favour he had gained away from me he fled.
He fled away like morning dew when the sun begins to shine,
And he quite forsook his Flora on the lovely banks of Boyne.

3. I understand this false young man to London took his way.
I gathered up my clothing all on that very day.
I bid farewell to my parents, I now in sorrow pine.
I forsook my father's castle on the lovely banks of Boyne.

4. I quickly pursued him unto fair London town,
Where there my love was married unto a lady of renown.
Young ladies, guess my feelings, I had to pain resign,
But he tempted me to wander on the lovely banks of Boyne.

5. Oh, alas, false memory brings to mind the days is past and gone,
And broken-hearted Flora, so far away from home.
Young ladies all be careful of how you pass your time,
And think on the fate of Flora on the lovely banks of Boyne.

The Keyhole in the Door

2. We left the parlour early, I'm sure 'twas scarcely nine,
And by a strange coincidence her room was next to mine.
I resolved, like old Columbo, new regions to explore,
And took up my observation at the keyhole in the door.

3. Then down upon the carpet, and kneeling on one knee,
My right eye to the keyhole, to see what I could see.
She first took off her collar, and it fell upon the floor.
I saw her stoop and find it through the keyhole in the door.

4. Oh, first this lovely maiden took off her pretty dress.
I spied her undergarments, some fifty, more or less.
To tell the truth exactly, I know there was a score,
But I couldn't count correctly through the keyhole in the door.

5. Then down upon the carpet she sat with graceful ease,
And pulled her snow-white garments above her lovely knees.
A dainty sky blue garter round either leg she wore.
It made a glorious picture through the keyhole in the door.

6. She then went to the fire, her pretty feet to warm,
With nothing but her chemise on I viewed her every charm.
Thinks I, "Take off that chemise and I'll ask for nothing more,"
By hell I seen her do it through the keyhole in the door.
Through the keyhole in the door, through the keyhole in the door,
By hell, I felt like jumping through the keyhole in the door.

Down by Yon Shady Harbour

You tender hearted lovers, come listen to my grief,
My darling's going to leave me in hopes of no relief.
All to some foreign island they've sent my love away,
For to obtain this fortune all in A-mer-i-ca.*

2. Then as I roved out one evening all in the month of May,
Down by yon shady harbour carelessly I did stray.
I heard two lovers talking, he thus to her did say,
"My darling, I must leave you and go to America."

3. "Oh Willy, dearest Willy, how could you prove unkind,
To a maid you loved so dearly, how could you change your mind.
For when you reach Columbia some other girl you'll see.
You won't think on your solemn vow that you have made to me.

4. "Oh Mary, dearest Mary, how could I prove unkind,
To a maid I loved so dearly, how could I change my mind.
There is no other fair one but you I do adore.
My daily thoughts will be of you while on Columbia's shore."

5. They kissed, shook hands, and parted, and home she did return,
Saying, "Willy, dearest Willy, oh, for your sake I'll mourn.
Because I was a servant girl, they send my love away,
For to obtain his fortune all in America."

6. This maid she then got ready without the least delay,
And now she's off to Belfast town her passage for to pay.
And when she got aboard of Josephine, those very words did say,
"Adieu, adieu, old Ireland, I'm for America."

7. Oh when she landed in America, providence proved kind.
The night and day bewailing, her Willy she could not find.
She walked out one evening, her Willy she chanced to see,
"You're welcome here, dear Mary, you're welcome here to me."

8. He took her in his arms and he thus to her did say,
"Our parents need not frown on us for we are far away.
Our parents need not frown on us for we are far away.
We'll join our hands in wedlock bands, all in America."

* pronounce A-Mary-Kay

The Dog and His Gun

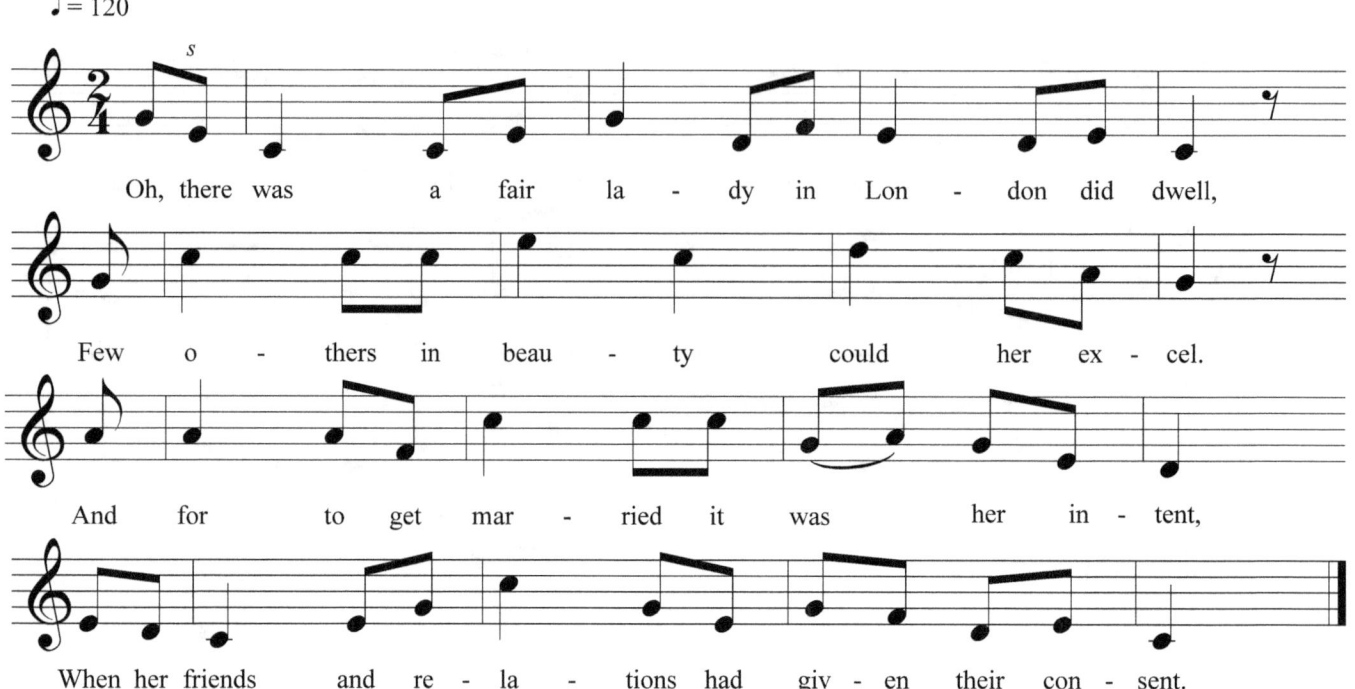

Oh, there was a fair lady in London did dwell,
Few others in beauty could her excel.
And for to get married it was her intent,
When her friends and relations had given their consent.

2. The day was appointed when she should be wed.
They chose a young farmer to wait on the bride.
But when the young lady the farmer espied,
He enflamed her heart, "Oh, the farmer," she cried.

3. Instead of getting married she went to her bed,
For the thoughts of the farmer so ran in her head.
A plan for to gain him she quickly did find,
As the thoughts of the farmer so ran in her mind.

4. Waist coat and britches next day she put on,
And she went a-hunting with her dog and her gun.
She hunted all around where the farmer did dwell,
For she knew in her heart that she loved him right well.

5. Oft times did she fire, but nothing did she kill,
Until a young farmer came into the field.
And for to converse with him it was her intent,
With her dog, and her gun to meet him she went.

6. "I thought you're at the wedding," the lady replied.
"To wait on the squire, and to give him his bride."
"Oh no," said the farmer, "the truth to you I'll tell,
I could ne'er give her away for I loved her too well."

7. It pleased the lady to see him so bold.
She gave him her glove that was flowered with gold,
Saying, "I picked it up while coming along,
As I was a-hunting with my dog and my gun."

8. Then for to try the young farmer his love,
She put it up in hand bills that she had lost a glove.
And when that he does find it and bring it to me,
I vow and declare his bride I will be.

9. When the young farmer he read of the news,
Straight to the lady he went with the glove,
Saying, "My dearest, honoured lady, I picked up your glove.
Now will you be so kind as to grant me your love."

10. "It's already granted," the lady she replied.
"For I love the sweet breath of a farmer," she said.
"I'll be mistress of my dairy and milking my cow,
As my jolly young farmer whistles after his plough."

11. The day of the wedding she told of the fun.
How she hunted up the farmer with her dog and her gun.
"And now since I have him so fast in my snare,
I'll enjoy him forever I vow and declare."

Erin's Lovely Home I

As I lay there a-waiting until my tri-al day,

My love, she came un-to the jail and this to me did say.

"Cheer up, my dar-ling Wil-ly, for you I won't dis-own,

Un-til you do re-turn a-gain to E-rin's love-ly home."

Erin's Lovely Home II

When I was young and in my prime, my age being twen-ty-one,
And I be-came a ser-vant un-to a gent-le-man.
I served him true and hon-est and ver-y well it's known,
By cru-el-ty he ban-ished me from E-rin's love-ly home.

2. The reason that he banished me I mean to let you know.
I own I loved his daughter, and she loved me also.
She had a large fortune, and riches I had none,
And that's the reason I must go from Erin's lovely home.

3. It was in her father's garden in the merry month of June,
We were picking of those flowers all in their youth and bloom.
She says, "My dearest Willy, if with me you will roam,
We'll bid adieu to all our friends in Erin's lovely home."

4. I gave consent that very night along with her to go,
Far from her father's dwelling which proved my overthrow.
The night being bright by the moonlight we both set out alone,
Expecting to get safe away from Erin's lovely home.

5. It was in a short time after, her father did appear
Which proved our sad misfortune as you will quickly hear.
He marched us back to Homer jail in the county of Tyrone,
Where there I was transported from Erin's lovely home.

6. I have seven links upon my chain, for every link a year,
Before I can return to the arms of my dear.
But when I do return again I will make her my own,
And we will live most happily in Erin's lovely home.

There Was an Old Woman

2. The old man took a toothache and the pain he couldn't endure.
She says, "I'll go to the doctor and I'll find you a cure."
chorus

3. She went to the doctor, a remedy to find.
She went to get something for to set the old man blind.
chorus

4. The old man took the remedy and threw it against the wall.
He says, "My dear old woman, sure, I can't see you at all."
chorus

5. He says, "I would go drown myself if I could find the way."
She says, "I'll go along with you, you shall not go astray."
chorus

6. So it's side by side they walked 'til they come to the river's brim.
He says, "Now take a running race and shove me headlong in."
chorus

7. So the old woman took a long running race to shove the old man in.
When he simply stepped aside and headlong she fell in.
chorus

8. She went down to the bottom and she came up to the brim.
He got a big long pole and he shoved her further in.
chorus

9. So now my song is ended and I mean to sing no more.
But wasn't my wife a silly old hag, she couldn't swim ashore.
chorus

By Borden's Grove

2. "Oh," she says, "young man, be civil, you compliments give o'er.
I made a vow, and I'll tell you now, it's seven long years or more.
My Johnny is on the ocean, and single I'll remain.
I'll wander alone through Borden's Grove 'til Johhny comes home again."

3. "Oh, what kind of a lad was your Johnny, what colour was his hair?
Likewise the ship he was sailing on, can you not tell me where?"
"He wore a short blue jacket, and his hair to his belt was tied.
Oh, my Johnny was a fine looking lad, and built to a clever size."

4. "If that be your love, Johnny, you shall never see him more.
He's gone on board the French Flattery where cannons they do roar.
He's gone on board the French Flattery where heroes they do fall,
And your Johnny lies a-bleeding, cut down by a cannonball."

5. "If that be so," young Mary cries, "this night I'll find no rest.
No tongue can tell the aching that lies all in my breast.
Through lonesome graves and willows, through valleys and through plains,
I'll wander alone through Borden's Grove, and die a blooming maid."

6. It was all for one love-making, and then her Johnny she knew,
And into his arms, right instantly she flew,
Saying, "You're welcome home, dear Johnny, since all your troubles are o'er,
And now since we've met in Borden's Grove we never shall part no more."

The Banks of Sweet Dundee

There was a rich merchant's daughter as I am lately told,
Her father died and left her five hundred pounds of gold,
She lived along with her uncle, that cause of all her woe,
And very soon now you shall hear how she did him overthrow.

2. Her uncle had a ploughboy who Mary loved so well.
'Twas in her father's garden they tales of love did tell.
There was a wealthy squire oft times came to her see.
Oh, but still she loved the ploughboy on the banks of sweet Dundee.

3. Her uncle he arose one morn I mean to let you know,
And straight to Mary's chamber door he instantly did go,
Saying, "Rise up, lovely Mary, a lady you shall be.
The squire is waiting for you on the banks of sweet Dundee."

4. "One fig for all your squires, your lords I don't surmise.
I would rather have my Willy, he's like diamonds in my eyes."
"Begone you faithless female, as married you ne'er will be.
I mean to banish Willy from the banks of sweet Dundee."

5. The press gang came on Willy when he was all alone.
He boldly fought for liberty but there was three to one.
The blood did flow in torrents, "Now kill me, now," said he,
"I'd rather die for Mary on the banks of sweet Dundee."

6. One evening as young Mary was wandering all alone.
She met this wealthy squire all in her uncle's grove.
He put his arms around her. "Stand off young man," cried she,
"You banished the only one I love from the banks of sweet Dundee."

7. The squire released her, and as he turned around
She spied a sword and pistol beneath his morning gown.
She took those weapons from him, the sword she used quite free.
She fired, and shot the squire on the banks of sweet Dundee.

8. Her uncle hearing of the noise, he hastened to the scene,
And when he saw the squire lying dead upon the green,
He turned, and looked at Mary, "You murderess." cried he,
She fired, and shot her uncle on the banks of sweet Dundee.

9. The doctor was sent for, the man of noted skill.
Likewise her uncle's lawyer to draw her uncle's will.
He willed all his gold to Mary who fought so manfully,
And closed his eyes no more to rise on the banks of sweet Dundee.

10. She wrote her love a letter all on that very day,
And told him to return without any more delay.
When he received the letter he returned right manfully,
And in wedlock bands they joined their hands on the banks of sweet Dundee.

My Good Looking Man

2. For when I was a blooming maid, a maid of sweet sixteen,
I looked upon a nice young man just about that time.
I looked upon a nice young man, to win him was my plan,
Soon after I got married to my good looking man.

3. We were scarcely three weeks married when one Sunday afternoon,
He walked out, and I walked out all in our honeymoon,
He walked out, and I walked out, to watch him was my plan.
When a lady gay I chanced to see with my good looking man.

4. They first shook hands, and then did kiss, and tales of love did tell.
Says I, "Me lad, when I get you home I'll tan your hide right well."
Says I, " Me lad, when I get you home I'll put you off your plan."
So I walked right home, no care to take of my good looking man.

5. Just as the clock was striking twelve my gentlemen walks in.
"Oh what has kept you out," says I, "Oh where have you been?"
"I was in church," says he. "You lie," says I, "is this your roguish plan?"
And the rolling pin I then let fly at my good looking man.

6. I scratched his face, I tore his hair, in ribbons I tore his clothes.
I then picked up a poker, and lay it across his nose.
He looked just like a chimney sweep as through the streets he ran,
But no lady gay has fell in love since with my good looking man.

7. Come all you married women, wherever you may be,
If you meet with a rakish husband pitch in to him like me.
My lad full thought to deceive me, so it was my only plan,
To disfigure the handsome countenance of my good looking man.

The Maid of Sweet Gurteen

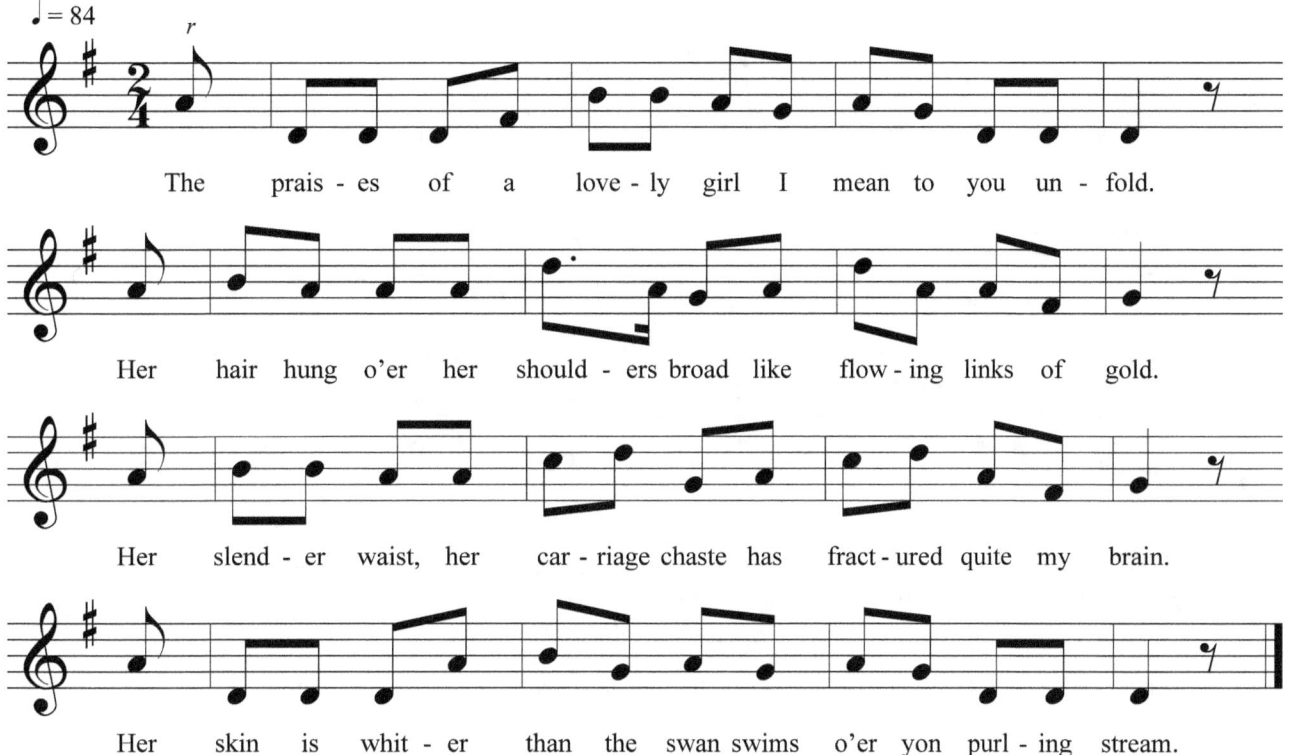

The prais-es of a love-ly girl I mean to you un-fold.
Her hair hung o'er her should-ers broad like flow-ing links of gold.
Her slend-er waist, her car-riage chaste has fract-ured quite my brain.
Her skin is whit-er than the swan swims o'er yon purl-ing stream.

2. So modest and so gentle, she was fit for any queen,
More gentle and more beauteous fair than I had ever seen.
The peaceful hours of time I have spent all in the garden green.
She has won my heart, I cannot part with the maid of sweet Gurteen.

3. My father he arose one morn, and this to me did say,
"Son, dear son, be advised by me, don't throw yourself away.
For to marry a poor servant girl whose parents are so mean,
So stay at home, and do not roam with the maid of sweet Gurteen."

4. "Oh father, dearest father, don't part me from my dear.
I would rather have my darling girl than a thousand pounds a year.
Were I possessed of King George's crown, of her I'd make my queen,
And in all the land I would wear the crown with the maid of sweet Gurteen."

5. My father in a passion flew, and this to me did say,
"Since that be the case, all in this place no longer shall she stay.
Mark what I say, from this very day you ne'er shall see her face,
For I'll send her far away from here unto some foreign place."

6. In two or three days after a horse he did prepare.
He sent my darling far away to a place I know not where.
I may go to my true love's room, or to the gardens green
In hopes to get another sight of the maid of sweet Gurteen.

7. Now to conclude and finish, I mean to end my song.
John O'Brien it is my name, Flower Hill it is my home.
I may go to my true love's room or to the gardens green,
But here in pain I now remain for the maid of sweet Gurteen.

The Gypsy Daisy

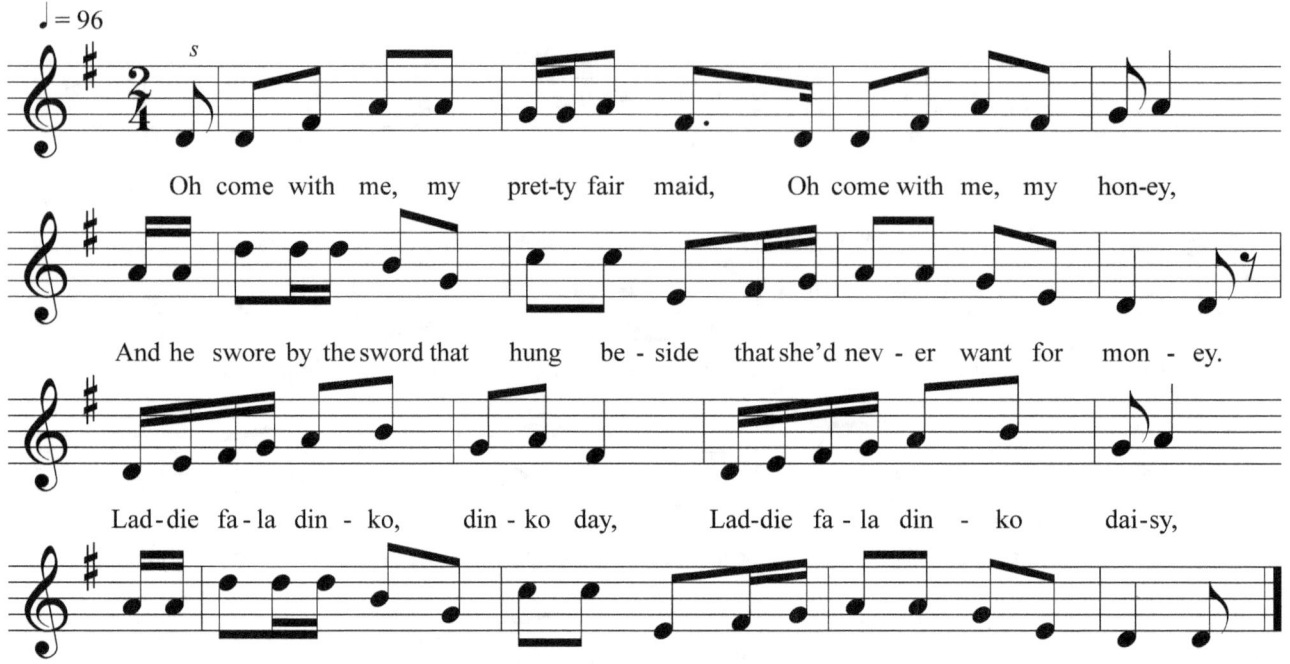

Oh come with me, my pretty fair maid, Oh come with me, my honey,
And he swore by the sword that hung beside that she'd never want for money.
Laddie fa-la din-ko, din-ko day, Laddie fa-la din-ko daisy,
And he swore by the sword that hung beside that she'd never want for money.

2. Her lord came home in the middle of the night enquiring for his lady,
When the servant girl made this reply, "She's gone with the gypsy daisy."
Laddie fa-la din-ko, din-ko day, laddie fa-la din-ko daisy,
When the servant girl made this reply, "She's gone with the gypsy daisy."

3. "Go saddle me my old grey steed, the bay is not so speedy.
I drove all day and I'll drive all night, 'til I overtake my lady."
Laddie fa-la din-ko, din-ko day, laddie fa-la din-ko daisy,
"I drove all day and I'll drive all night, 'til I overtake my lady."

4. He drove along by the water's edge, the water it being muddy,
And from each eye a tear trickled down when he espied his lady.
Laddie fa-la din-ko, din-ko day, laddie fa-la din-ko daisy,
And from each eye a tear trickled down when he espied his lady.

5. "Last night I lay on a warm feather bed that was both soft and easy,
And tonight I lie on the damp, cold ground with a band of gypsies round me."
Laddie fa-la din-ko, din-ko day, laddie fa-la din-ko daisy,
"And tonight I lie on the damp, cold ground with a band of gypsies round me."

The Mower

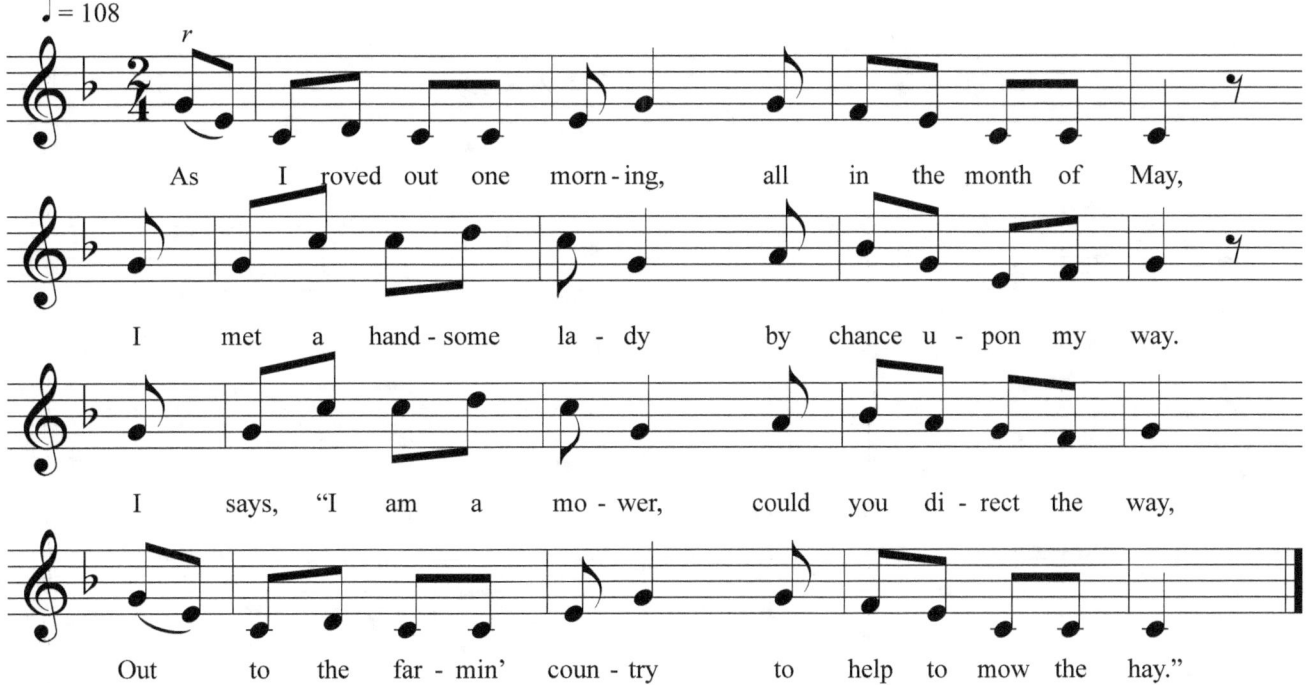

2. "Oh, if you be a mower, and a mower be your trade,
Perhaps you might some mowing find among so many maids.
I have a little meadow, it's a long time kept in store,
It's like the dew that's in Peru, 'twas never touched before."

3. With courage bold, undaunted, I marched into the field,
I mowed from nine to dinner time, and I was forced to yield.
I mowed from nine to dinner time, I mowed beyond my skill,
I was forced to yield, and quit the field, the grass was growing still.

4. "Oh, now I have your meadow mowed, and I must go away,
All to some foreign country to help to mow the hay.
And if the hay be all cut down in the country where I go,
Perhaps I might return again your meadow for to mow."

5. "Oh, Jimmy, don't you leave me, nor from me go away.
You promised that you'd marry me at the mowing of me hay.
'Twas in that little meadow, you found no hills nor rocks,
So I pray, young man, don't leave me 'til you see my hay in stocks."

The Farmer's Son and the Shantyboy

As I roved out one evening just as the sun went down,
So carelessly I wandered down by the riverside.
I heard two maids conversing as slowly I passed by.
One said she loved a farmer's son and the other a shanty-boy.

2. Oh, the one that loved the farmer's son those words I heard her say,
"The reason that I love him, at home with me he'll stay.
He'll stay at home all winter, to the wild woods he won't go,
And when springtime rolls around again he'll plough the fields and sow."

3. "Oh, for the ploughing, and sowing the lands," the other girl did say.
"I don't think much of business that's carried on that way.
Your crops they prove a failure, and the grain market being low,
The bailiff then will sell you out to pay the debts you owe."

4. "Oh, for the bailiff selling us out, it does not me alarm.
We grow our bread from off our land, don't work through squalls, and storm.
We grow our bread from off our land, don't work through hail, and rain,
While the shantyboy has to work each day, his family to maintain."

5. "Oh, how I praise my shantyboy that goes out in the fall.
He's hardy, stout and willing, can weather any squall.
With pleasure I embrace him in the spring when he comes home.
His money free he'll share with me when your farmer son's got none."

6. "Oh, how you praise your shantyboy that goes out in the fall.
He's ordered out before daylight to work through squalls, and storm
While happy, and contented with my farmer's son am I.
Sweet tales of love he'll tell to me 'til the storm it does roll by."

7."Oh, how I hate that soft talk your farmer's sons do say.
Why some of them, they are so green that the cows might eat for hay.
It's easily to know them when they go into town.
The small boys up to them do run saying, 'me, and are you down'."

8. "All that I said about your shantyboy, I did not mean it so.
If ever I meet with one of them along with him I'll roam.
If ever I meet with one of them along with him I'll go.
I'll leave the habitants with broken hearts, their fields to plough and sow."

Skibbereen

"Oh father, I often hear you talk of Erin's lovely isle,
You said it was a handsome place, so rich and rare the soil.
You said it was a lovely place where any prince might dwell,
Oh, why then did you abandon it, the reason to me tell."

2. "Oh son, I loved my native home with honour, and with pride,
These pleasant valleys where I roamed, those meadows long, and wide.
Throughout those rich green valleys where I wandered as a boy,
My shamrock, and shillelagh was my constant pride and joy.

3. But oh, a blight came o'er my crop, my sheep, and cattle died,
And when the rent it was to pay, I no longer could provide.
Oh, well do I remember that dark November day
When the landlord, and the sheriff came to drive us all the way.

4. They set our roof a-blazing with scornful bitter spleen,
And when it fell, the crash was heard all over Skibbereen,
Your mother too, God rest her soul, lay on the snow white ground.
She fainted in her anguish at the desolation round.

5. She never spoke, but passed away amidst the tumultuous scene,
And found a silent resting place in dear old Skibbereen.
My son, you're scarce two years old, and feeble was your frame.
I would not leave your friends while you bore your father's name.

6. I wrapped you in my old fur coat in the dead of night unseen,
I hove a sigh, and bid good-bye to dear old Skibbereen."
"Oh father dear, the day will come when for freedom we will call,
When Irishmen in Ireland will rally one and all.

7. I'll be the man to lead the gang beneath Erin's flag of green,
And low, and high we'll raise the cry of dear old Skibbereen.
I'll be the man to lead the green beneath Erin's flag of green,
And low and high we'll raise the cry of dear old Skibbereen."

By the Rosy Banks So Green

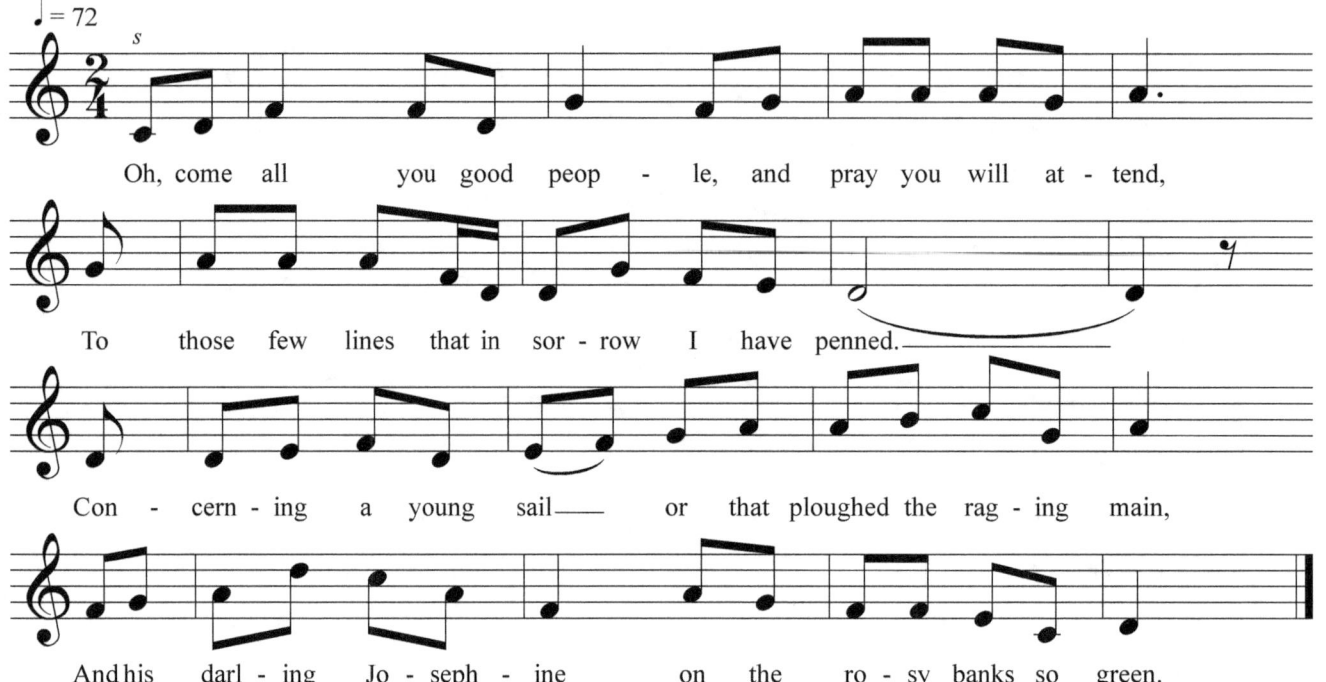

Oh, come all you good people, and pray you will at-tend,
To those few lines that in sor-row I have penned.
Con-cern-ing a young sail — or that ploughed the rag-ing main,
And his darl-ing Jo-seph-ine on the ro-sy banks so green.

2. It was on a summer's evening down by her uncle's grove,
This lady sat conversing with a lad she dearly loved.
A-kissing, and embracing, he cried, "Dear Josephine,
This night we will be far from the rosy banks so green."

3. Her old father overheard them, 'til he could no longer stand.
He rushed upon those lovers with a loaded gun in hand.
Saying, "Die you cursed youth, no more you plough the main,
For this night I'll separate you on the rosy banks so green."

4. He aimed the deadly weapon, the fatal trigger drew.
Josephine like lightning to her lover's arms she flew
But the fatal ball had sped its course, so true had been its aim
That they fell side by side on the rosy banks so green.

5. As young Josephine lay dying, those words I heard her say,
"It's well that my old mother did not live to see this day.
From a high seat in glory a witness she has been,
To the murdering of her daughter on the rosy banks so green."

6. As young Willie he lay dying, those words I heard him say,
"Soon we will be lying in a cold and silent grave."
He embraced her in anguish, and kissed both cheeks, and chin.
They did die side by side on the rosy banks so green.

7. "Oh, fare you well, dear Willie, no more you will return,
To your poor old aged mother who will never cease to mourn.
But you'll rise up in glory with your own dear Josephine,
And you'll never be forgotten on the rosy banks so green."

8. Oh come all you good people, I pray you will draw near,
To the graves of those young lovers, and in silence shed a tear.
For beneath the marble tombstone, down by the purling stream,
Lie those innocent young lovers on the rosy bank so green.

The Hat My Father Wore

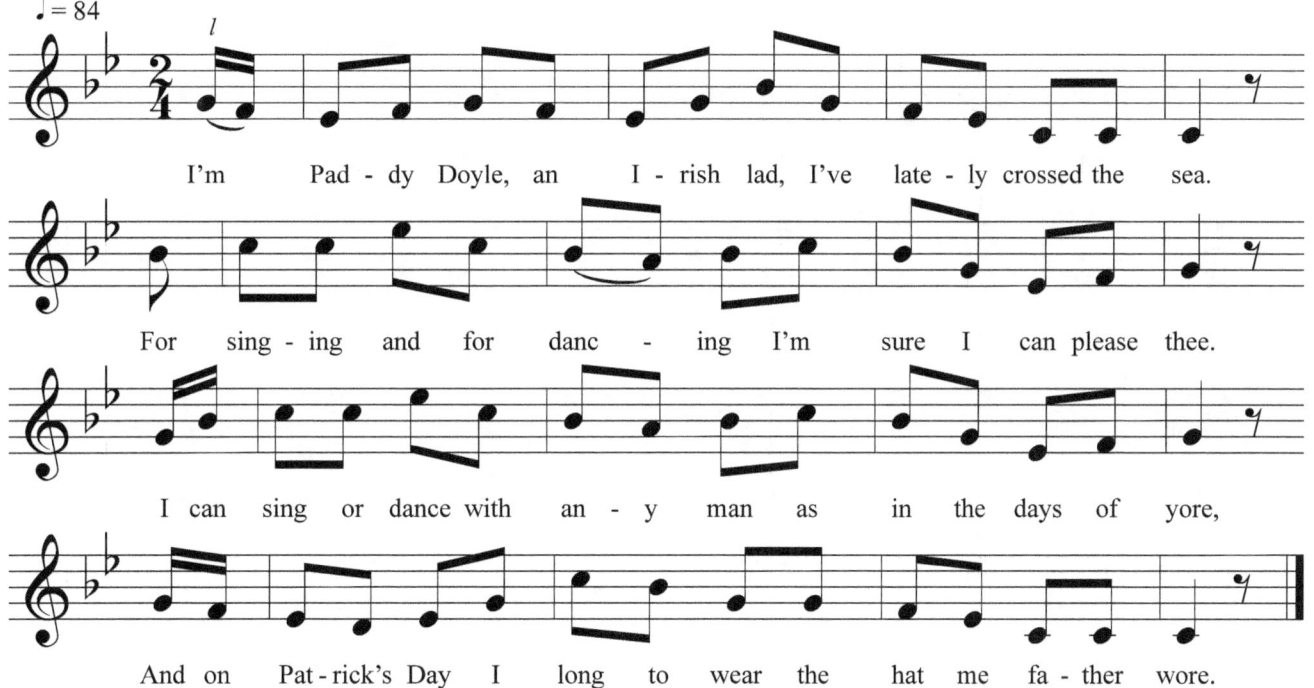

2. It's old, but it's beautiful, it's the best you've ever seen.
It's been worn for more than ninety years on that little isle so green.
For on me father's great ancestors, it descended in the lore,
And on Patrick's Day I long to wear the hat me father wore.

The Lass of Glenshee

2. Her cheeks were like roses adorned with a dimple,
And bright was the beam of her bonny blue eye.
Her face was enchanting, her form neat and handsome,
My heart soon belonged to the lass of Glenshee.

3. I stepped up to her, says I, "Fairest creature,
If you will but come to Caledonia with me,
There's no one but you shall step forth in my castle,
Nor none shall be clothed more costly than thee.

4. Believe me, fair creature, Caledonia's bright waters,
Shall alter their course, and turn back from the sea.
The bright gleaming sun will be bound down in fetters,
E're I ever prove false to me charming Jennie.

5. Oh, sit down beside me, and don't talk so lightly,
Should bullets fly round me, my bride you shall be.
This night in my arms, oh, so fondly I'll treat you,"
She smiled, and consented, I took her with me.

6. It's seven long years, oh, since we were united,
There's many a change since, but no change in she.
My love is as pure as the rose that in winter,
Lies out, and gets withered on the hills of Glenshee.

On the Banks of the Don

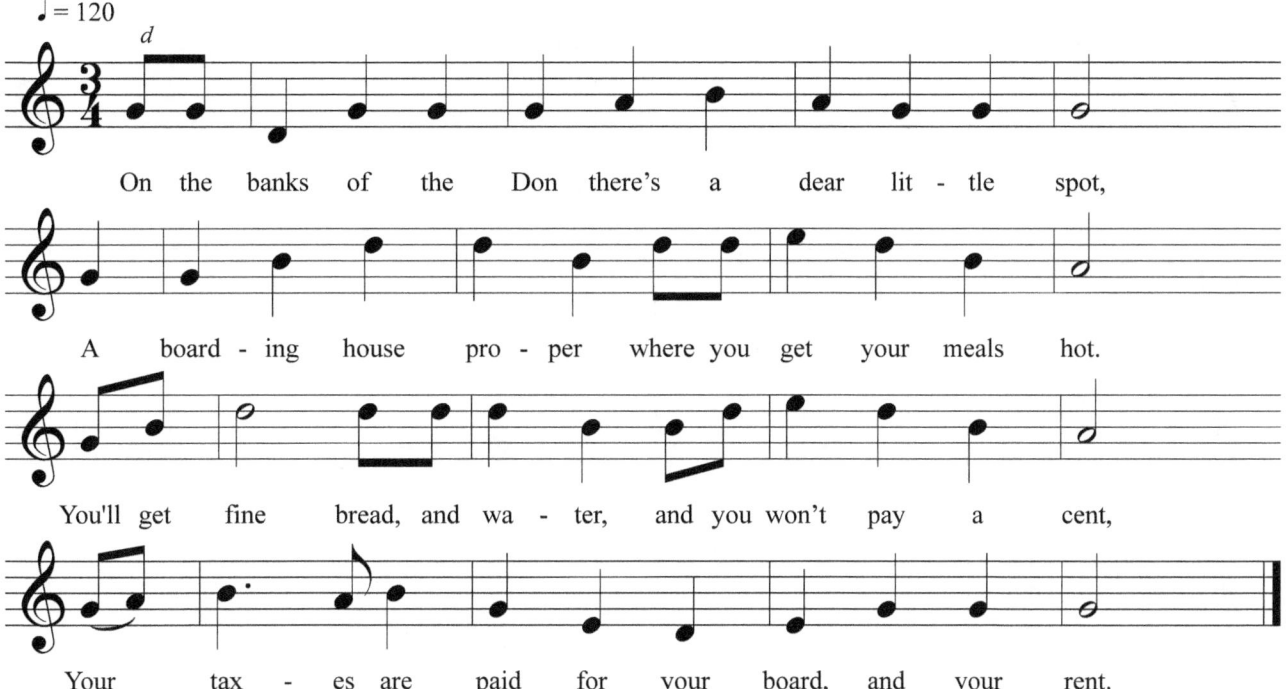

On the banks of the Don there's a dear little spot,
A boarding house proper where you get your meals hot.
You'll get fine bread, and water, and you won't pay a cent,
Your taxes are paid for your board, and your rent.

2. So turn out every men of you all in a line,
From the cell to the stone yard you all must keep time.
You'll work like a Turk 'til the bell it strikes one,
In the grand institution just over the Don.

3. If you want to get into that palace so neat,
Take Tanglefoot whiskey, and get drunk on the street.
You'll have a fine family carriage to drive you to town,
To the grand institution just over the Don.

4. Our boarders are honest, not one of them steal,
For we count all our knives and forks after each meal.
Our windows are airy, and barred up besides,
To keep our good boarders from falling outside.

5. So turn out every man of you all in a line,
From the cell to the stoneyard you all must keep time.
You'll work like a Turk 'til the bell it strikes one,
In that grand institution just over the Don.

Lost Jimmy Whelan

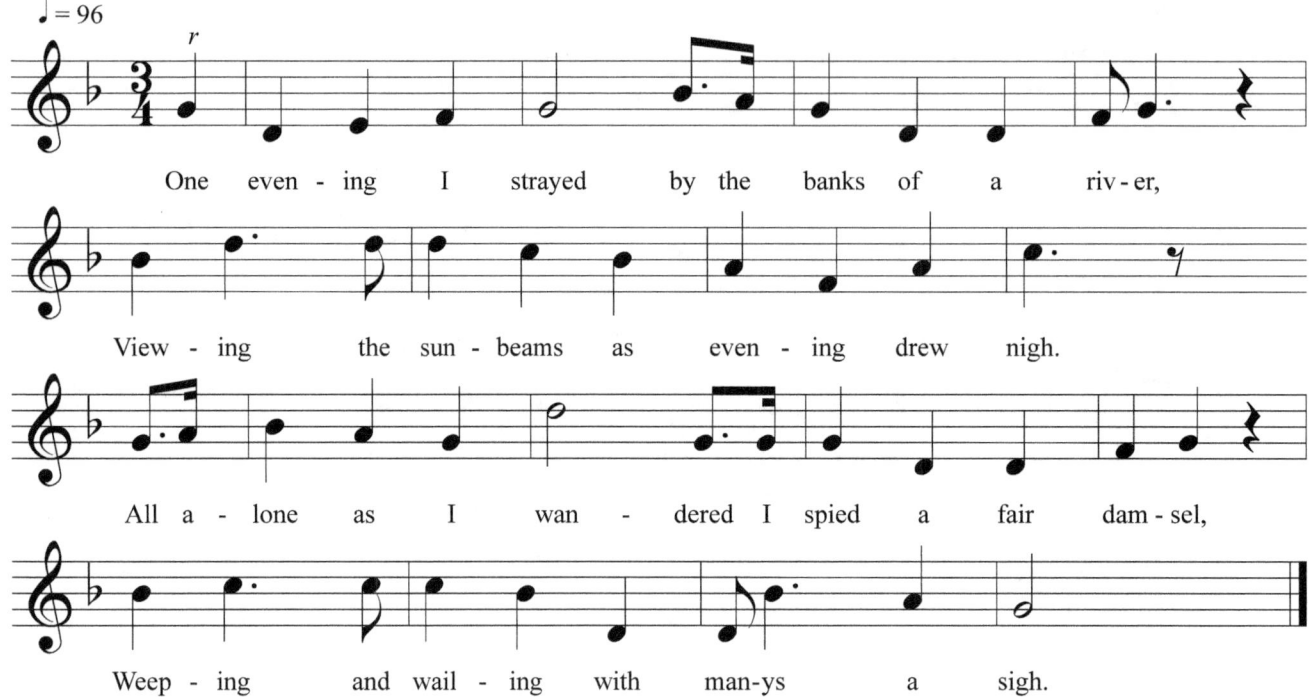

One evening I strayed by the banks of a river,
Viewing the sunbeams as evening drew nigh.
All alone as I wandered I spied a fair damsel,
Weeping and wailing with manys a sigh.

2. Sighing for one who is now lying lonely,
Weeping for one who no mortal could save.
For the cold cruel waters flow sadly around him,
As onwards they flow over young Jimmy's grave.

3. "Oh, Jimmy," she says, "won't you come to my arms.
Come to me, Jimmy, from your silent grave.
You promised you'd meet me this evening, my darling,
But death's cruel anger has sealed your sad fate.

4. You promised you'd meet me by the banks of this river,
To give me sweet kisses as you oft did before,
To enfold me again in your strong loving arms.
Come to me, Jimmy, oh come from your grave."

5. Up he arose from the depths of the water,
A vision of beauty more bright than the sun.
Realms of crimson surrounded young Jimmy,
And unto this fair one to speak he began.

6. "Oh why did you call me from realms of glory,
Back to this world where I'll soon have to part."
Cold were the arms that did her encircle,
And cold was the bosom he pressed to her heart.

7. "All alone as you wander by the banks of this river,
I will be with you to guard, and to save.
My spirits will hover, and keep you from danger
'Til death takes you down to your cold, silent grave."

8. Throwing herself on the ground she wept sorely,
With great words of anguish this maiden did rave,
Saying, "Adieu, oh adieu, my lost Jimmy Whelan,
I'll sigh 'til I die by the side of your grave."

As I Roved through an Irish Town

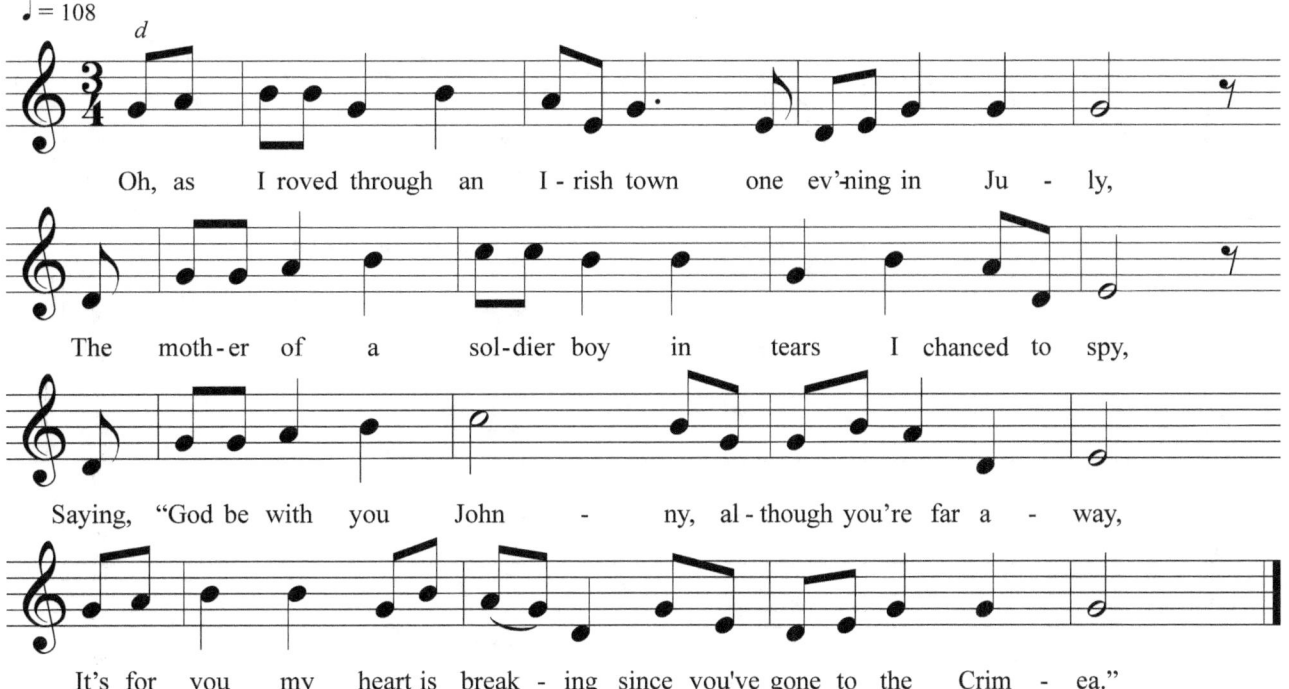

2. "Oh Johnny, I gave you schooling, I gave you a trade likewise,
You need not have joined the army had you took my advice.
You need not go to fight the foe where the thundering cannons roar,
And where thousands lay a victim all on the Russian shore."

3. Oh, we joined the 14th regiment, it was a splendid core,
Landed safe as man should upon the Russian shore.
We fought in four engagements with a loss of men each day.
Oh, my darling mentions all to me, although he's far away.

4. Oh, when we fought at Balaclava where we did not succeed,
Likewise the battle of Inkerman where thousands fell indeed.
We fought at Cashalarma with a loss of men each day
Oh, my darling mentions all to me, although he's far away.

5. Oh, when we attacked Sebastopol, it was there you'd see some play,
The very ground we stood upon, it shook unto the sea.
The clouds look black with heavy smoke, and bombshells firing there,
And thousands falling on the plains that went to fight the bear.

6. Oh, the battering of Sebastopol it did the world surprise.
Hard it was to take it, the enemy being so wise,
But the Paddy's sons, and British guns their valour did display,
And together with the men of France, thank God, we gained the day.

7. Now to conclude and finish, I mean to end my song.
I thank the Lord that protected me for to survive so long.
It's God be with my Mother for it's me she does adore,
I hope I'll live to see her in Garryowen once more.

I'll Write You a Letter

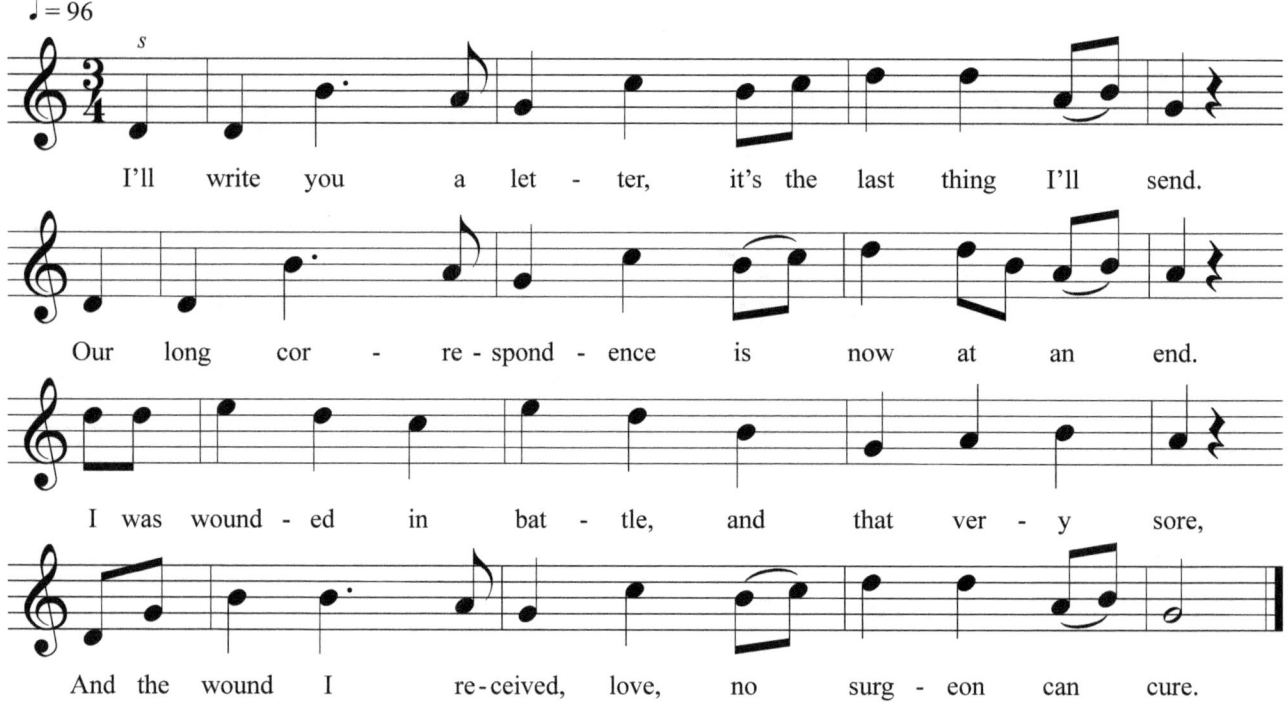

I'll write you a letter, it's the last thing I'll send.
Our long cor - re-spond - ence is now at an end.
I was wound-ed in bat - tle, and that ver - y sore,
And the wound I re-ceived, love, no surg - eon can cure.

2. As I write you this letter I lie on the ground,
The blood from my wounds like a fountain flows down.
With my knapsack I stopped it to gain as much time,
As would write you a letter, you sweet darling of mine.

3. The last time we parted it gave me great pain,
We were in fond hopes of meeting again.
But our fond hopes are all over, we shall ne'er meet no more,
Farewell, lovely Annie, you're the girl I adore.

Tommy and the Apple

As Tom-my was walk-ing one fine sum-mer day,
Some ro-sy cheeked ap-ples he saw on his way.
Saw on his way, saw on his way,
Some ro-sy cheeked ap-ples he saw on his way.

2. Those apples were ripe, and so pleasant to see,
They seemed to say, "Tommy, come climb up the tree.
Come climb up the tree, come climb up the tree,"
They seemed to say, "Tommy, come climb up the tree."

3. So Tommy climbed up, from the bough he did fall,
And down came poor Tommy, the apples, and all.
Apples, and all, apples, and all,
And down came poor Tommy, the apples, and all.

4. His face was all scratched, and he felt very sore,
He promised he'd never steal apples no more.
Apples no more, apples no more,
He promised he'd never steal apples no more.

Pat O'Donnell

2. We sailed on board the ship *Wild Rose* in August '83,
And on my maiden voyage to Cape Town he was unknown to me.
When I found out he was a Carey we had angry words, and blows,
The villain strove to take my life on board the ship *Wild Rose*.

3. I stood up in my own defence to fight before I die.
My cocked pistol I pulled out, and at him I did fly.
I fired at him the second time which pierced him through the heart,
And I gave him a third volley boys, before from him did part.

4. His wife and son came running down to the cabin where he lay.
When they saw him in his dying gore, it filled them with dismay.
"Pat O'Donnell, you shot my husband," Mrs Carey aloud did cry.
"Oh yes, I did in my own defence, kind woman," then said I.

5. The captain had me hand-cuffed, and in strong irons bound.
He had me taken prisoner when we landed in Cape Town.
They marched me back to London where my trial did come on,
The prosecutors for my crime was Carey's wife and son.

6. Oh, the jury brought my verdict and the judge my sentence passed.
I was tried for willful murder, and guilty found at last.
"For the shooting of James Carey," the scornful judge did cry,
"On the seventeenth of November, Pat Donnell, you must die."

7. There's one request I ask of you, and that, before I go,
Let no man think that Carey fell by a cowardly treacherous blow.
For the hand that knocked the traitor down would fain to banish more,
And all false, and foreigners from that sainted Irish shore.

8. And if I was a free man to live another year,
All traitors and informers, I would make them shake with fear.
Like St. Patrick drove the serpents from that sainted Irish ground,
I would make them fly before me like a hare before a hound.

9. Adieu, adieu, a long farewell, this is our parting day.
I hear the death bell tolling, good Christians for me pray,
And to the blessed virgin on bended knee do fall,
For the soul of Pat O'Donnell from the County Donegal.

The Colleen Bawn

2. But the girl I love is beautiful, she's as gentle as a fawn,
She dwells in Limerick city, and she's called the Colleen Bawn.
Just as swiftly as that river flows through that far famed city,
Just as coolly, and without a word, my Colleen passes me.

3. Oh, if I were made the emperor, all Russia to command,
Julius Caesar, or the Lord, lieutenant of the land,
I'd get my crown down off my head, my people on their knee,
Likewise a fleet of sailing ships out on the briny sea.

4. I'd give the crown down off my head, my people on their knee,
Likewise a fleet of sailing ships out on the briny sea.
A beggar I would go to bed, and happy rise at dawn,
If by my side, all for a bride, I'd find the Colleen Bawn.

The Dying Girl

You may raise the window, moth-er dear, no breeze can harm me now,
Let the breeze blow un-ob-struc-ted, it will cool my fev-ered brow.
Death soon will end my suf-fering, soon will ease my ach-ing heart.
I have a dy-ing message I must speak e'er I de-part.

2. There is one, you know him, mother dear, I need not tell his name,
You know how he sought me, by those tender words he came,
'Til he gained my affection, it was by love's gentle tone
That he would forever love me, and someday make me his own.

3. Do not chide him, mother dear, though you miss me from your side,
For I wish him every happiness with one so soon his bride.
Gladly I'll receive the summons to go to that happy land,
Where no heart was ever lonely, but all for the holy band.

4. You know how much I trusted, putting all my thoughts in him.
You may raise the window, mother, for the light is growing dim.
You know, too, how he used me cool, by putting me at one side,
And how he chose another fair one for to be his bride.

5. Take that ring from off my finger where he placed it long ago.
Give it to him as a token that, undying, I bestow,
Give it to him as a token of forgiveness, and of peace,
For I think my joy, and happiness in this world soon will cease.

6. You may raise the window, mother, I am growing colder now.
Mother, wipe the perspiration from off my fevered brow.
Hark, I hear my Savior calling, 'tis his voice, I know it well.
Mother, meet your child in heaven, one fond kiss, and then farewell.

Barney Blake

My name is Barney Blake, I'm a tearing Irish rake,
Considered by the neighbours sort of handy.
I was reared up in the spade, and I learned the tailoring trade,
I think meself as good as Mick or Sandy.

chorus
Biddy Donahue, I have got my eye on you,
If you'll only marry Barney, you'll have no cause to rue.
You're the apple of my eye, I'm your conquering Irish boy,
Cupid knocked me stupid for my charming Donahue.

2. I'm a cosmopolitan swell, contented anywhere,
Contented at my daily occupation.
I courted a Colleen rue called Miss Biddy Donahue,
She is the pride of all the Irish nation.
chorus

3. 'Twas at the wedding of Pat O'Hare, I first met Biddy there,
As she sat beside me at the wedding supper.
When she handed me me tea, how I felt I couldn't say,
But my heart, it melted like a lump of butter.
chorus

4. I asked her there and then if she'd have me for her man,
She smiled at me as cute as any jailer.
She answered "yes" with pride, and since that I'm satisfied,
She'll have no one else but Barney Blake the tailor.
chorus

5. Some livery boy seemed to try for to knock out Barney's eye,
But soon they will find it a failure.
She will not see Barney fooled, she's as pure as guinea gold,
To her humpin', jumpin', stumpin' Irish tailor.
chorus

My Charming Sally Ann

Oh, when I was young, and boy-ish my mind was full of glee,
I roamed about with pleasure, and from every care was free,
'Til I fell in with a charming girl, and then my life began.
I pitched head over heels in love with me charming Sally Ann.

2. The first place that I saw her it was at a gay old spree,
Her eyes, they shone like diamonds bright, oft times she winked at me.
As I returned her glances, her features I would scan,
I got as crazy as a bed bug after charming Sally Ann.

3. I went to her house one evening, and I met her at the door.
I discoursed with her old mother for most an hour or more.
The old lady talked quite sensible saying, "I'll do the best I can,
To make you hunky-dory with my daughter Sally Ann."

4. I went to her house another evening and the old folks weren't within,
I saw some strange performances there which almost made me grin.
My love was frying sausage for Bob the butcher's man,
And I asked an explanation from me charming Sally Ann.

5. She flew into a passion saying, "Boys what do you mean?"
Says I, "Me charming Sally, I'm not altogether green."
Those words were scarcely spoken 'til she gripped the frying pan,
And you'd laugh to see the sidelips of my charming Sally Ann.

6. I asked her for the jewellery that I had given to she.
She flew into a passion, like a wildcat she did purr,
Saying, "You made me of them presents when you were the dense young man,
So leave the house, you savage," cried my charming Sally Ann.

7. On my way home I met a police, and my story to him did tell,
I gave him a gold dollar which seemed to please him well.
Back to Sally's there we went, and around the house we ran,
But the devil a fragment could we find of my charming Sally Ann.

8. On my way home I met the old man, and my story to him did tell,
That Sally Ann had run away with Bob, the butcher's man.
The old man he vowed vengeance on Bob, the butcher's man,
And the old lady she vowed vengeance on her daughter Sally Ann.

9. Well, like railroad speed, the old man did drive a splendid span of greys.
He cracked his whip and swore by oath in the good old-fashioned way.
We were not long a-driving 'til we saw another span,
And very soon we overtook me charming Sally Ann.

10. The policeman in the scrimmage, sure he got a broken thigh,
The old man with his cudgel he poked out the butcher's eye.
Sally and her mother, they tore hair, hand by hand,
But she couldn't hold a candle to her daughter Sally Ann.

The Barley Grain for Me

2. Then the farmer came with a big plough, we ploughed me under the sod,
Sure the barley grain shot forth his head with a beard like any man.
chorus

3. Then the reaper came with a sharp hook, he made me no reply,
He caught me by the whiskers, and cut me above the thigh.
chorus

4. Then the binder come with her neat thumb, she bound me all around,
And then they hired a handyman to stand me on the ground.
chorus

5. Then the pitcher came with a sharp fork, he pierced it through me heart,
And like a rover or highwayman, they bound me on the cart.
chorus

6. Then they took me to the barn, and spread me out on the floor,
They left me there for a space of time, and me beard grew through the door.
chorus

7. Then they sold me to the brewer, and he brewed me on the pan,
But when I got into the jug I was the strongest man.
chorus

8. Then they drank me in the kitchen, and they drank me in the hall,
But the drunkard used me worse, he bashed me agin' the wall.
chorus

Cooper and Donnelly

Oh, come all you true born Irishmen, I hope you will attend,
I hope you'll pay attention to those few lines I've penned.
It's all as true a story as ever you did hear,
About Cooper, and brave Donnelly who fought all on Kildare.

2. It was on the third of June, me boys, a challenge was sent o'er
From Brittania to old Grania to renew her sons once more.
To renew her satisfaction, her credit to recall,
They are all in deep distraction since Donnelly conquered all.

3. Oh, the challenge was accepted, and those champions did prepare,
To meet brave Captain Kelly on the currow of Kildare,
From six to nine they fought that time, first Donnelly knocked him down.
Old Grania smiled, "Well done, my child, that win one thousand pounds."

4. Oh, the very next round that Cooper fought, sure he knocked Donnelly down,
Those Englishmen they gave three cheers while he lay on the ground.
And Cooper being quite active, he knocked Donnelly down once more,
Those Englishmen, they gave three cheers, saying, "The battle he may give o'er."

5. Oh, long life to brave Miss Kelly, she's recorded on the plains.
She boldly stepped into the ring saying, "Dan, what do you mean?
Oh, Dan," says she, "what do you mean, Hibernia's son," said she,
"My whole estate, I have it bet, that you will win the day."

6. "Oh, be not afraid, Miss Kelly," he says as he lay on the ground,
"You may bet your coach, and horses, likewise ten thousand pounds.
It's do not fret for I ain't bet although I've got two falls.
I'll let them know before I go that Cooper'll pay for all."

7. "I am not afraid," Miss Kelly says, "but you will gain the day,
My coach and four I freely bet upon you Donnelly.
You are a true born Irishman as gentry well does know,
So on the plains of sweet Kildare, this day your valour show."

8. Then Donnelly rose most furiously, and meeting with great might,
For to stagnate his nobles, he continued to the fight.
Cooper stood in his own defence, exertion proved in vain,
He soon received a temple blow that stretched him on the plain.

9. "Now you sons of old Britannia, your boasting now give o'er,
It's by our hero Donnelly, your champion is no more.
Out of eleven rounds, took nine knock downs, besides broke his jaw bone,
Shake hands with me brave Donnelly, the battle it is now o'er."

A Bunch of Watercresses

Oh, I am a dairy farmer, from Belveshire I came,
To see some friends and relations, and Morgan is my name.
If you will sit and listen, I'll tell without delay,
Of a pretty little damsel my attention stole away.

2. It was on the first of April when I arrived in town,
And being quite a stranger I rambled up and down.
'Til I lost myself entirely, I cannot tell you where,
'Twas a very quiet place near the corner of a square.

3. When a neatly dressed young maiden came walking up that way,
As long as I remember I shall never forget the day.
She promised she would marry me upon the first of May,
And she left me with a bunch of watercresses.

4. Oh, politely I addressed her, and this to her did say,
"I want to go to Camberwell, can you direct the way?"
"Oh yes, sir, oh yes, sir," she modestly replied,
"Take the turning to the left, and then go down the other side."

5. Her voice it was the sweetest that ever I did hear,
Her hands were like the lily, and so very white, and clear.
She had some early onions, a half a pint of beer,
Some pickles, and a bunch of watercresses.

6. I bowed to her, I thanked her, I passed by her side,
I thought how neatly she would look as a dairy farmer's bride.
So I gathered resolutions, half in earnest, half in joke,
I hinted matrimony, those are the very words I spoke.

7. "I've a farm of forty acres, stocked with horses, cows and geese,
Besides I have a dairy house of butter, milk and cheese.
Kind maiden, would you marry me, and be mistress of all these,
And we'll spend our days in loving watercresses."

8. "Oh yes, sir, oh yes, sir, oh dear if you choose,
You are so very generous, I cannot well refuse.
I've a wedding dress to buy, and some little bills to pay,"
I handed her a sovereign, her expenses to defray.

9. Next day a letter I received I read it with surprise,
"Kind sir, for disappointing you I must apologize.
But next time you ask a stranger into partnership for life,
Be sure that she's a maiden or a widow, not a wife.

10. I've a husband of my own and his name is Willy Gray,
And when I can afford it, your sovereign I will pay.
But to think that I would marry you upon the first of May,
Why you must have been as green as watercresses."

The Lonesome Scenes of Winter

2. Oh, one night as I went up to see my love she proved more scornfully,
I offered fair to marry her, she would not hear to me.
The night is almost past and gone, 'tis near the break of day,
"Oh, and all I want is an answer, my dear, what do you say?"

3. "Oh well, kind sir, since I must answer you, I cannot be your wife,
It's lately I have chosen to lead a different life.
You may go some other where, and for yourself provide,
I have got another suitor, and you I'll lay aside."

4. Oh well, since this lady I loved has changed her mind to lead a different life,
I will go some other where in search of as handsome a wife.
I will go some other where for love must have its fill,
This world is wide and lonesome if one doesn't, another will.

5. Oh, some people boast of pleasure, but I no pleasure see,
The small birds they are singing most sweet from tree to tree.
The small birds they are singing most lovely and divine,
Oh, and all I want is an answer, my dear will you be mine.

The Drunkard's Dream

Oh, Dermott you look healthy now, your dress more neat and clean,
I do not see you drunk about, come, tell me where you've been.
Your wife and family are all well, you once did use them strange,
But you are kinder to them now, how come the happy change?

2. It was a dream, a warning voice, which Heaven sent to me,
To snatch me from a drunkard's curse, grief, want, and misery.
My wages were all spent in drink, oh, what a wretched view,
I almost broke my Mary's heart, and starved my children too.

3. "I dreamt one night I staggered home, what means this awful gloom,
Where is my wife, where can she be, and strangers in the room."
I heard them say, "poor thing, she's dead, she has led a wretched life,
His grief and want has broke her heart to be a drunkard's wife."

4. I seemed like one all in a trance, then rushed to where she lay,
I bent and kissed her pale, cold lips, forever cold as clay.
"Speak, Mary, once again," I cried, "no more I'll cause you pain,
No more I'll cause those eyes to weep, or ever drink again."

5. When I awoke my Mary dear was kneeling by my side,
I pressed her to my throbbing heart while tears fell from our eyes.
I pressed her to my throbbing heart while tears of joy did stream,
And ever since I've Heaven blessed for sending me that dream.

Home, Green Erin, O

2. Oh, it's Luther sweet spring roads you'll find that blooms on our green isle,
And if we desired the blood to spill it sorely us beguile.
'Til clergy flocks through groves and rocks to preach were forced to go,
And to leave that lovely fertile isle called home, green Erin, O.

3. Oh it's hard to part with any land, the land you love so well,
It's hard to part with parent dear, it's more than tongue can tell.
It's hard to part with my sweetheart, the girl I love, you know,
But it's harder still, against my will, to part green Erin, O.

4. Here's to my honoured parents that live at home in Newell,
But when I sleep on the ocean deep my sorrows are oppressed.
But when I reach Columbia I'll wander to and fro,
But my thoughts the same will still remain for home, green Erin, O

My Bonny Irish Boy

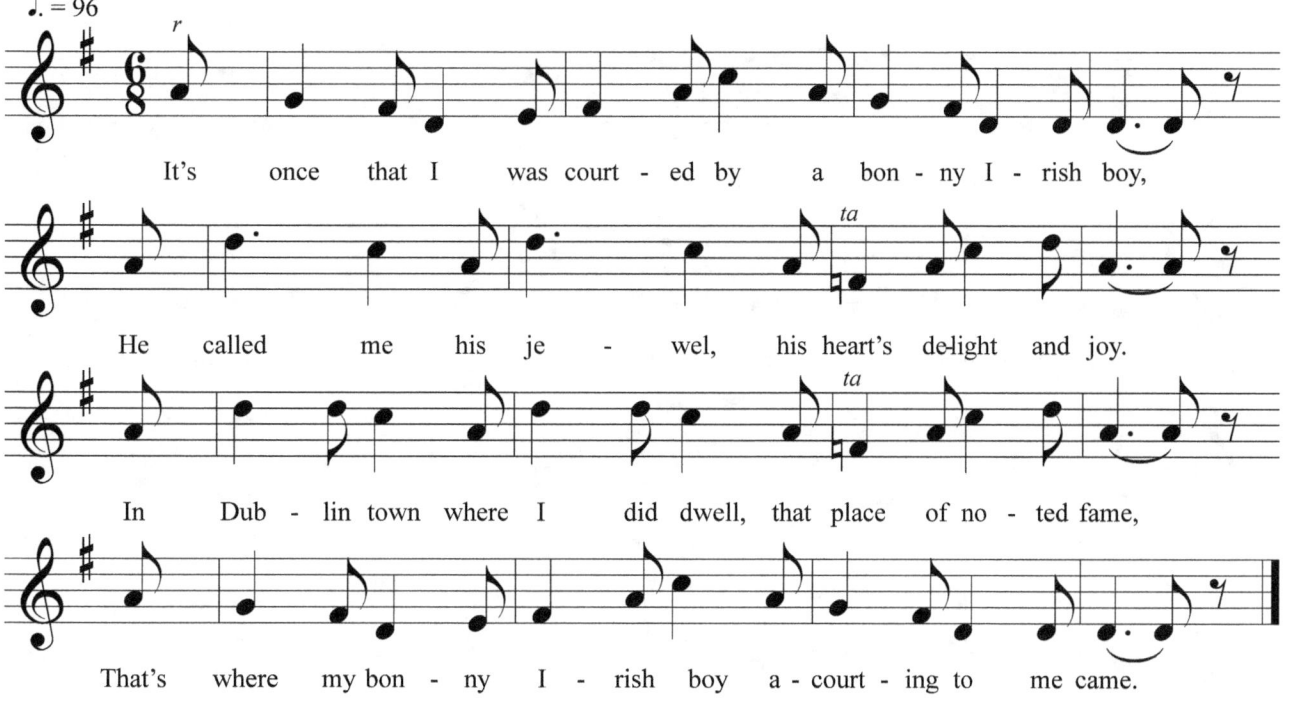

The Green Linnet

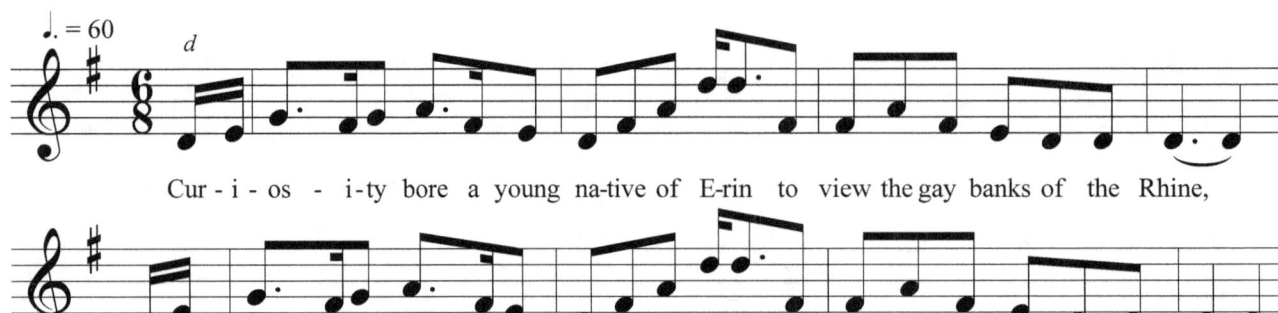

2. The cold, lofty Alps you freely went over
      which nature had placed in your way,
   That Marengo Saloney all round you did hover,
      all Paris rejoiced the next day.
   It grieves me, the hardships that you did undergo
      or mountains you travelled all covered with snow,
   The balance of power your courage laid low,
      are you gone, will I e'er see you more.

3. That numbers of men are eager to slay you
      their malace you viewed with a smile.
   Their goal through all Europe, they sought to betray you,
      and joined with the Mamelukes on the Nile.
   Like ravens for blood their vile passions did burn,
      orphans they slain, and left widows for to mourn.
   They say my linnets gone, will he ever return
      oh, sweet Bony, will I e'er see you mourn?

4. I will roam through the desert of wild Abyssinia,
      and yet find no cure for my pain.
   Will I go and inquire at the Isle of St. Helena?
      Oh no, we will whisper in vain.
   Tell me, ye critics, oh, tell to me in time,
      or the world I'll range o'er, my green linnet for to find?
   Was he slain at Waterloo, the Elbe, on the Rhine?
      If he was I shall ne'er see him more.

Note: *The Battle of Marengo was a decisive French victory of Napoleon's campain in Italy in 1800. Mamelukes were a powerful group of Turkoman warriors who ruled in Egypt under Ottoman sovereignty until they were defeated in 1811.*

Daniel O'Connell

Oh, you lover's of mirth, I pray pay attention, and listen to what I am going to relate,
Concerning a couple I overheard talking as I was returning late home from a wake.
As I roved along, I spied an old woman who sat by the gap all a-minding her cow,
She was jigging a tune called, "Come Haste to the Wedding," or some other ditty I can't tell you now.

2. Though in looking around I spied a bold tinker, who only by chance came strolling the same way.
The weather being warm, he sat down to rest, "Ah, what news, honest man?" the old woman did say.
"Then it's no news at all, ma'am," replied the bold tinker, "but on, and I wish that he never had been,
It's that damnable rogue of a Daniel O'Connell, he's now making children in Dublin by steam."

3. "Are the children a rue?" replied the old woman, "O hainm an diabhail*, is he crazy at last?
Is a sign of a war or a sudden rebellion, or what is the reason he wants them so fast?"
"Then it's not war at all, ma'am," replied the bold tinker, "but the children of Ireland are getting so small.
It's O'Connell's petition to the great Lord Luftman to not let us make them the old way at all."

4. "Oh, by this pipe in me mouth," replied the old woman, "and that's a great oath on my soul for to say.
I'm only a woman and if I were near him, I'd bet you my life he'd have little to say.
Sure the people of Ireland it's very well known that they gave him their earnings though needing it bad,
And now he is well recompensing them for it by taking what little diversion they had."

5. "Oh, long life to you woman," replies the bold tinker, "and long may you live, and have youth on your side,
But if all the young girls in old Ireland were like you, O'Connell might pitch his steam engine aside,
And I think every one that is in this country should begin making children as fast as they can,
So if ever her majesty asks for an army, we'd be able to give them as many as Dan."

Note: *O hainm an diabhail is a Gaelic expression meaning "O in the name of the devil"*

A Man You Don't Meet Every Day

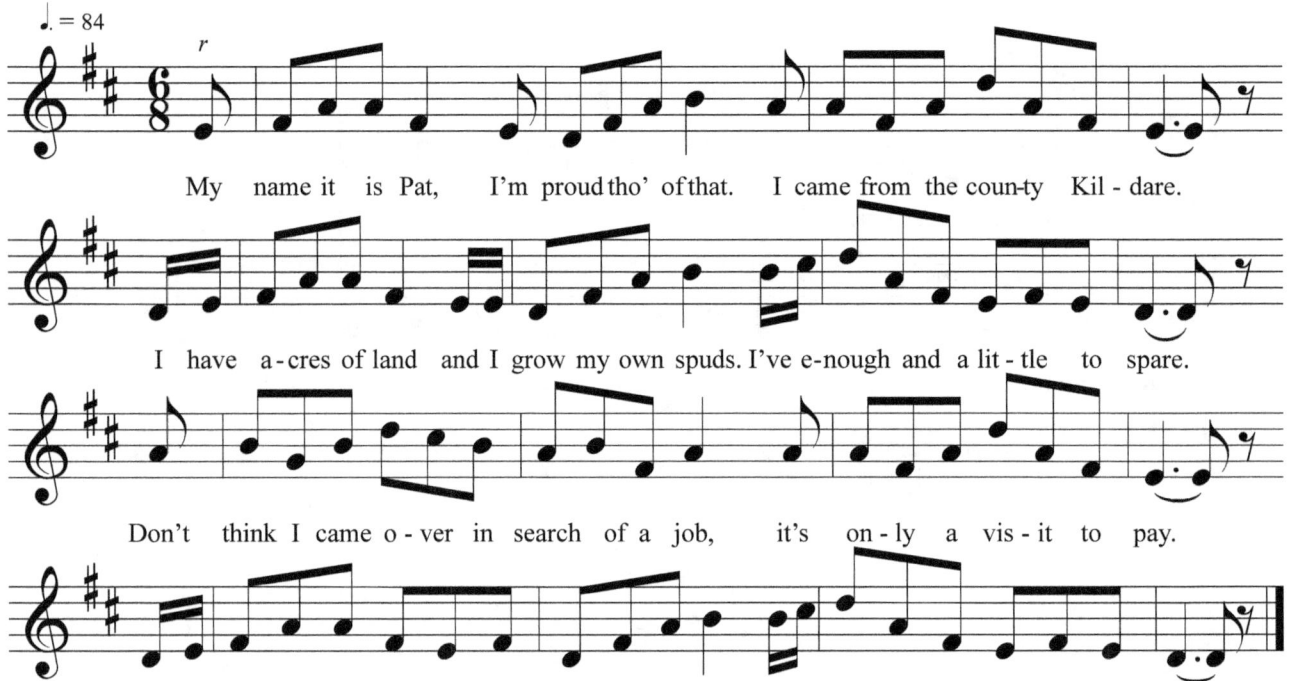

My name it is Pat, I'm proud tho' of that. I came from the coun-ty Kil-dare.
I have a-cres of land and I grow my own spuds. I've e-nough and a lit-tle to spare.
Don't think I came o-ver in search of a job, it's on-ly a vis-it to pay.
So be e-asy and free while you're drink-ing with me, I'm a man you don't meet e-very day.

2. When I landed in Liverpool, what a sight met my eyes as I gazed on the shore,
There was Paddy McGee and young Paddy Moore, Mike McFamous and one or two more.
They all burst out laughing when they seen myself walking, those words unto them I did say,
"Oh, be easy and free when you're drinking with me, I'm a man you don't meet every day."

3. One evening while walking I thought I had time, so I took a stray down to the store,
Who should I see there but young Paddy Moore with his glass of best ale at the bar.
I spoke to him kindly, took him by the hand, those words unto him I did say,
"So be easy and free when you're drinking with me, I'm a man you don't meet every day."

4. I've a neat little Colleen that lives about town, it's her I came over to see,
We're going to get married next Sunday and then she'll come back to old Ireland with me.
And if you come over a year from today, there's one thing I'll venture to say,
We'll have a wee lad that will say to his Dad, "Here's a man you don't meet every day."

Over the Mountain

I was al-ways light-heart-ed and air-y,— not a care in this world have I,
Be-cause I am loved by a Col-leen,— I could not for-get if I tried.

Chorus:
She lives far a-way o'er the moun-tains where I know she's still think-ing of me,
It's o-ver just o-ver the moun-tain where a lit-tle bird sings on the tree,
Éi-re cuis-le mo chroí* were I with you, how hap-py this mo-ment I'd be.
In a cab-in all co-vered with i-vy,— my El-i is wait-ing for me.

2. The day I bid goodbye to Eli, that day I will never forget
How the tears trickled down from their slumber, I fancy I can see them yet.
She looked like a pearl in the ocean as she whispered a fond tear of love,
Saying, "Eli my, boy, don't forget me, 'til we meet again here above."
Chorus:

3. True lovers often are parted, friends like flowers come and go,
But the face of my Eli will cheer me no matter wherever I go.
The instinct of love and devotion surrounded by thoughts chaste and pure
Will serve as a guide for the sailor when ploughing the wild raging morn.
Chorus:

Note: Eli pronounced "eelee"

*Éire cuisle mo chroí: Gaelic meaning Ireland, pulse of my heart

The Blackwater Side

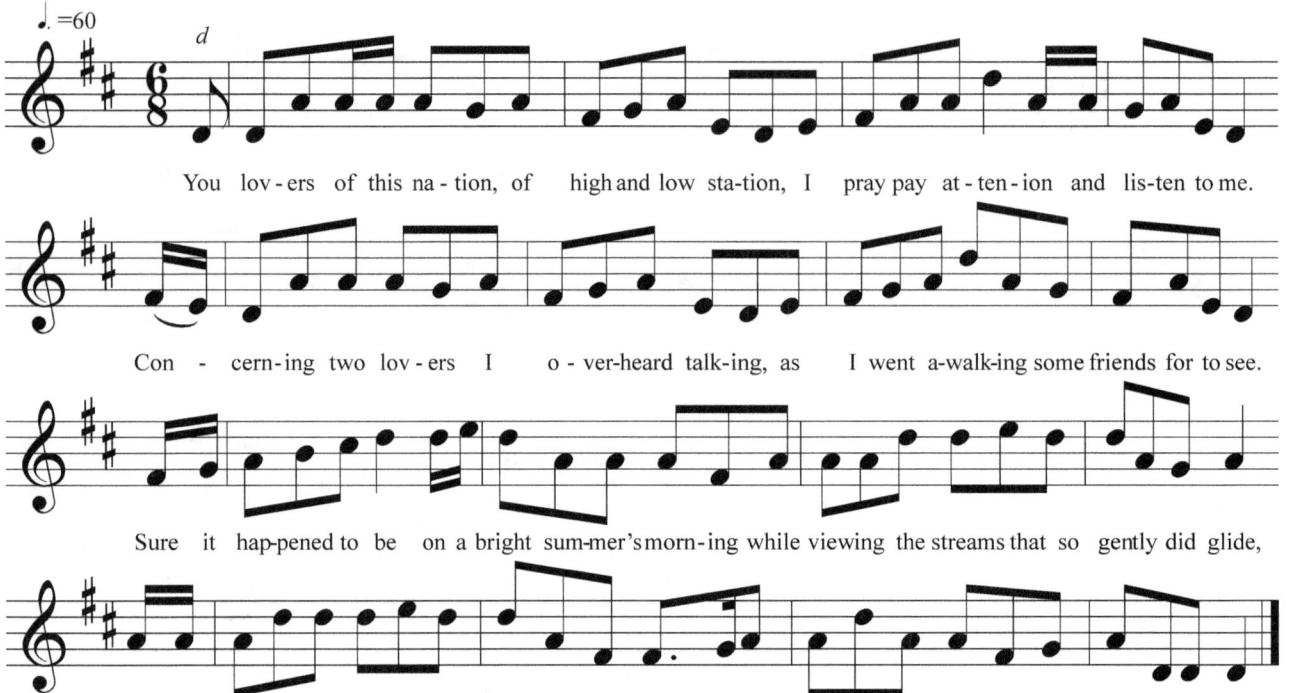

2. He says, "My true lover, we're long enough courting, we are both fit for marriage I solemnly vow.
And if you will agree, in wedlock to join me, either aye, yes or no, you must answer me now.
I want no hesitation, but come without waiting, I'm willing, and ready to make you my bride.
You're the maid I admire, grant me my desire, on the lovely green banks of the Blackwater side."

3. She says, "My true lover, the truth I'll discover, I'm quite unprepared for to answer you yet,
My fortune is low as you very well know, and to be your bride don't you know I'm not fit.
My clothing is bare, I have nothing to spare, I've worked very hard since my old father died,
Wait a year or two more and I'll go along with you, and we'll leave all our friends on the Blackwater side."

4. He says, "My true lover, the truth I'll discover, straightway I'll go with some other young fare,
As for your fortune, you know I disregard it, and for your clothing, I'm sure I don't care.
If she's comely and fair at the age of eighteen, I am willing, and ready to make her my bride,
You know I adore you, I chose none before you, my blooming sweet maid on the Blackwater side."

5. Then this lady arose, to her mother she goes, and told her her story as plain as may see,
She gave her consent, and straightway they both went, and in the sweet bands of wedlock, and unity joined.
May their welfare increase, and their sorrows grow less, in the sweet bands of wedlock may they always abide,
And mind I am telling that you'll find their dwelling on the lovely green banks of the Blackwater side.

The Banks of the Dee

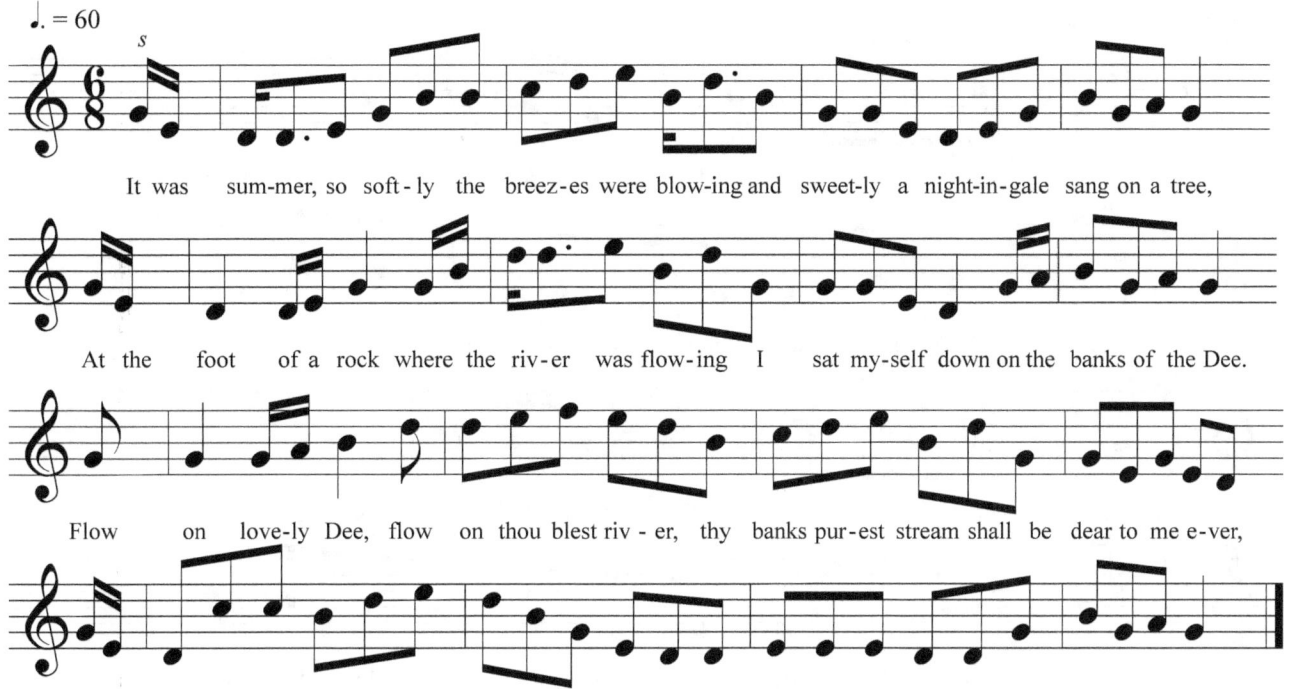

2. But now he has gone, he has left me this morning to quell the proud rebel, so valiant was he,
And there is no sign of his speedy returning, to wander again on the banks of the Dee.
He is gone, hapless youth, o'er the wild raging billows, the sweetest, and kindest of all those brave fellows,
And he has left me to wander among these green willows, the loneliest maid on the banks of the Dee.

3. But time, and prayer, oh, may it restore him, blest peace may restore my dear shepherd to me,
And when he comes back with such care I'll watch o'er him, he'll never again quit the banks of the Dee.
The Dee it will flow, all its beauties displaying, the lambs on its banks shall again be seen playing.
Whilst I with my Jimmy will be carelessly straying, and tasting again all the sweets of the Dee.

The Black Bottle

2. Oh, my heart gave a flutter, my two eyes did stare, says I, "You black villain, what's keeping you there?"
Oh, my heart gave a flutter, my two eyes did stare, says I, "You black villain, what's keeping you there?"
Up spoke the black bottle saying, "What's taking me off, sure I am pursued by the temperate stuff.
I am driven and banished from my own abode, and I'm left here alone for to die on the road."

3. "No," says I, "you black villain, I'm glad of your woe, for many's the time you have treated me so.
"No," says I, "you black villain, I'm glad of your woe, for many's the time you have treated me so.
You often have caused me to ramble the street, took the shirt off me back and the shoes off me feet,
The streets for to ramble, my bones you've left sore, the shirt on my back into ribbons you've tore."

4. Up spoke the black bottle, saying, "Keep good guard on your tongue, you never have spoke of good deeds I have done,"
Up spoke the black bottle, saying, "Keep good guard on your tongue, you never have spoke of good deeds I have done,
For when death calls upon you, your days for to end, it's for my assistance you're glad to ascend.
I am a physician, this world I've came through, and I am esteemed by far greater than you."

5. Oh, says I, "Me black villain, my mother that's dead, well do I remember the words that she said,"
Oh, says I, "Me black villain, my mother that's dead, well do I remember the words that she said,
You were her companion by night, and by day, and you were a good help to take her away."
Up spoke the black bottle, to me said, "I am much surprised that your mother is dead,
But if she was taken by sickness or pain, sure that is no reason I should bear the blame,
If the truth it was known, sure the fault was her own, she would not stay from me, nor leave me alone."

6. So I picked him up as he lay on the ground, and into my throat, sure I tumbled him down.
So I picked him up as he lay on the ground, and into my throat, sure I tumbled him down.
The lad wasn't long in the cellar below until he commenced to threaten me woe,
And for my misconduct he would have revenge, and ten times he nearly knocked out me brains.

7. Now, I've took an oath, on the Book I have swore, never to meddle with grog any more,
But the next time I go on a neat little jog, sure I hope they'll send down a shower of grog.

Note: *This song is written in eight phrases because of the length of the lines. However, it is basically A ABA form. In verse 5 O. J. Abbott repeated the B and A phrases. In verse 7 he sang only the A phrase.*

Terrence's Farewell

Oh, so Kathleen, you're going to leave me, all alone by myself in this place,
But I know you will never deceive me, Oh no, for there's truth in your face.
But England's a beautiful country, full of elegant boys, ah, what then?
You would not deceive your poor Terrence, you'll come back to old Ireland again.

2. Oh, those English are deceivers by nature, though it's maybe you'll think them sincere,
They'll say you're a charming sweet creature, but don't you believe them my dear.
E'er a Kathleen O'Grath don't be minding, whatever fine speeches they'll make,
Just tell them a poor boy in Ireland is breaking his heart for your sake.

3. Oh, there's no use to keep you from going, though faith, it's a mighty hard case,
For Kathleen O'Grath there's no knowing when next I will see your sweet face.
And when that I do see you, Kathleen, what better will I be off then?
You'll be speaking such beautiful English, sure I won't know my Kathleen again.

4 Ach, now what's the use of the hurry, don't fluster me so in this way,
I've forgot between the grief, and the flurry, every word I was meaning to say.
Now just wait a minute I bid ye, can I talk if you bother me so?
My blessing go with you, dear Kathleen, every inch of the way that you go.

Old Erin

The Farmer's Boy

As the sun went down be-hind a cloud, as the drea-ry night was o'er,
Poor and lame there came a boy up to a far-mer's door.
Say-ing, "Please tell me a man about here that would me em-ploy,
To plough, to sow, to reap and mow, to be a far-mer's boy."

2. "My father's dead, my mother lives with her five children small,
And what is the worst for mother dear, I'm the eldest of them all.
Although I'm small, I fear no work if you'll only me employ,
To plough, to sow, to reap, and to mow, to be a farmer's boy."

3. "Oh well," said the farmer, "we'll try the lad, no longer have him seek,"
"Oh yes, dear Papa," his daughter cried, as the tear rolled down her cheek.
"For a lad that can work, it's hard for him to want, and to wander for employ,
Don't send him away, but let him stay, and be your labouring boy."

4. As the years rolled on, the boy grew up and the good old farmer died,
He willed to the lad the farm that he had, and his daughter for a bride.
And the lad that was once, he's a farmer now, and he often thinks with joy,
On the happy, happy day he came that way, to be a farmer's boy.

Captain Colstein

You in-hab-i-tants of Ire-land that's bound to cross the sea,
Come join with Cap-tain Col-stein that he-ro brave and free.
Come join with Cap-tain Col-stein that he-ro brave and bold,
Who fought his way a-cross the sea and ne-ver was con-trolled.

2. From the eleventh 'til the twenty-first we ploughed the raging sea.
For ten long days of merriment, bound for America.
Our merriment being over, and going to bed at night,
Our Captain went all around the deck to see if all was right.

3. "Oh, don't go down," our captain cried, "there is no time for sleep,
For in less then half and hour, we'll be slumbering in the deep.
The pirate ship is coming from up the wide western sea,
To rob us of our property, bound for America."

4. The pirate ship came up to us, and bid us for to stand.
"Your gold, and precious loading this moment I demand,
Your gold, and precious loading this day resign to me
Or not a soul will you ever bring into America."

5. Then up spoke Captain Colstein, that hero brave, and bold,
"It's in the deep we all shall sleep before we'll be controlled."
'Twas then the battle it began, the blood in streams it flowed.
Undaunted was our passengers, even the pirates was overthrown.

6. There was a lady on the deck with her true love by her side,
With courage bold she fought her way along the bulwark side,
Saying, "Don't you fret my bonny boy, we'll shortly end the strife,"
And with the pistol ball she took the pirate captain's life.

7. The cries of women and children whilst in the hold they lay,
Our captain and his passengers, they showed them Irish play,
The pirate ship surrendered just at the dawn of day,
And we marched them back as prisoners into America.

Note: America is pronounced "A-Mary-Kay."

The Banks of Newfoundland

Oh, ye may bless your happy lots, all ye who dwell on shore,
For it's little you know of the hardships that we poor seamen bore,
For it's little you know of the hardships that we were forced to stand
For fourteen days and fourteen nights on the banks of Newfoundland.

2. Our ship she sailed through frost and snow from the day we left Quebec,
And if we had not walked about, we'd have frozen to the deck.
But we, being true born sailormen as every ship had manned,
Our captain doubled our grog each day on the banks of Newfoundland.

3. There never was a ship, my boys, that sailed the western sea,
But the billowy waves came rolling in and bent them into staves.
Our ship, being built of unseasoned wood and could but little stand,
The hurricane it met us there on the banks of Newfoundland.

4. We fasted for three days and nights, our provisions giving out,
On the morning of the fourth day we cast our lots about.
The lot it fell on the captain's son, thinking relief at hand,
We spared him for another night on the banks of Newfoundland.

5. On the morning of the fifth day no vessel did appear,
We gave to him another hour to offer up a prayer.
But providence to us proved kind, kept blood from every hand,
For an English vessel hove in sight on the banks of Newfoundland.

6. We hoisted aloft our signal, they bore down on us straightway,
When they saw our pitiful condition, they began to weep and pray.
Five hundred souls we had on board the day we left the land,
There's now alive but seventy-five on the banks of Newfoundland.

7. They took us off of the wreck, my boys, we were more like ghosts than men,
They fed us and they clothed us and brought us back again.
They fed us and they clothed us and brought us safe to land,
While the billowy waves roll o'er their graves on the banks of Newfoundland.

By the Hush, Me Boys

2. Then I sold me horse, and plough, me little pigs, and cow,
And me little farm a land, then I parted.
And me sweetheart Biddy McGee, I'm a-feared I'd never see,
For I left her that morning broken hearted.
Chorus

3. Then meself, and a hundred more to America sailed o'er,
 Our fortune to be making we were thinking.
When we landed to Yankee land, shoved a gun into our hand,
Saying, "Paddy, you must go and fight for Lincoln."
Chorus

4. General Mahar, too, is said, "If you get shot or lose your head,
Every murdered soul of you will get to pension."
In the war I lost me leg, all I've got now is a wooden peg,
By me soul, it is the truth to you I mention.
Chorus

5. Now I think meself in luck to be fed upon Indian buck,
In old Ireland, the country I delight in.
And with the devil I do say, "Curse America,"
For I'm sure I've got enough of their hard fighting.
Chorus

Note: America is pronounced "A-Mary-Kay."

The Soldier's Farewell

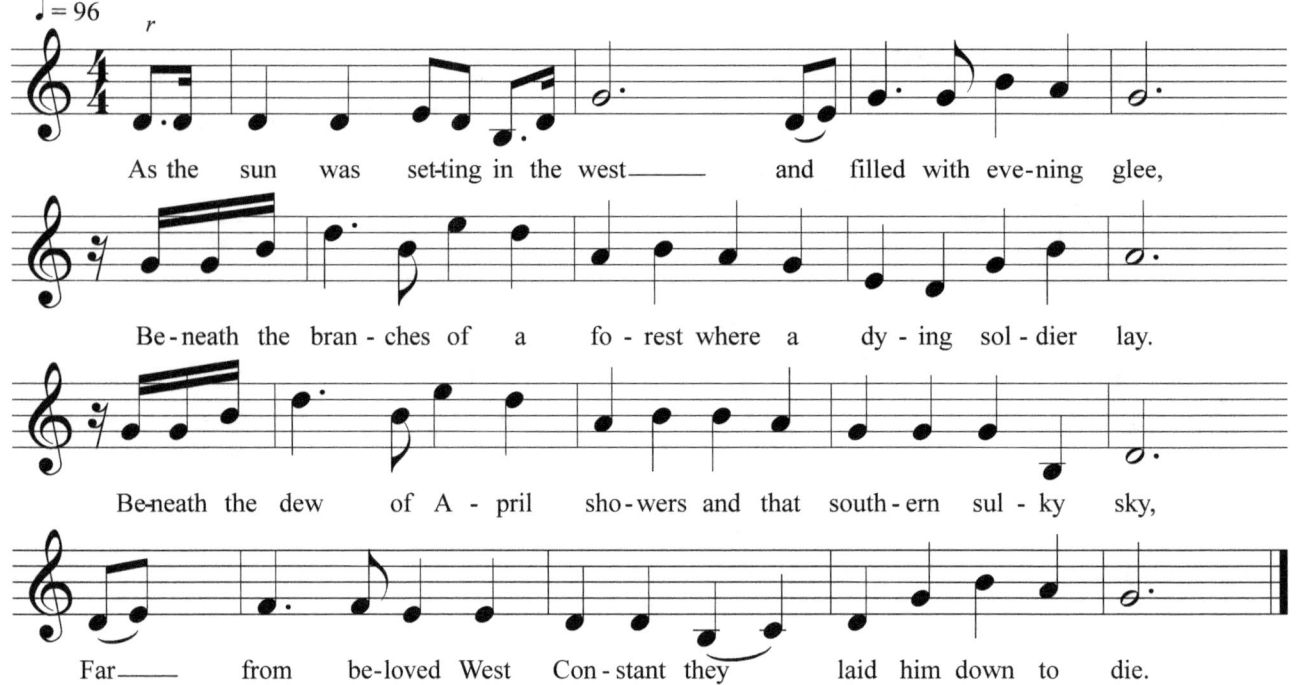

As the sun was setting in the west and filled with eve-ning glee,
Be-neath the bran-ches of a fo-rest where a dy-ing sol-dier lay.
Be-neath the dew of A-pril sho-wers and that south-ern sul-ky sky,
Far from be-loved West Con-stant they laid him down to die.

2. A group had gathered round him, his comrades brave, and true,
The tears rolled down his manly cheeks as he bid this world adieu.
Oh comrades gather closer, and listen to what I say,
'Tis a story I will tell you e'er my spirits passed away.

3. "Far away in beloved West Constant beneath the pine tree at the gate,
There is one who for my coming with a throbbing heart does wait.
It is my own dear sister, my joy, my only pride,
She was my joy in boyhood days, for I had none beside.

4. Tell my sister not to weep for me, nor sob with drooping head,
When the troops are marching home again with glad, and gallant tread.
But to look upon them kindly with a calm, and steadfast eye,
For her brother was a soldier too, and not afraid to die."

5. When our country was invaded, and called for volunteers,
She threw her arms about my neck, and in a flood of tears.
Says, "Go, my beloved brother, drive those traitors from our shore,
My heart, it needs your presence, but our country needs it more."

6. His comrades gathered closer to take the last farewell,
Of as true, and brave a soldier boy as ever in battle fell.
Far away from beloved West Constant they laid him down to rest,
With his knapsack for a pillow, and his sword on his breast.

Note: *While O. J. Abbott clearly sings "West Constant" the song is referring to West Connaught, a province on the west coast of Ireland.*

The Bonny Bunch of Rushes Green

As— I roved out one May morning to the green fields I took my way,
With my two beagles roaring, expecting there some game to see.
It was there I spied my Mary, she was fairer than Arabian queen,
She was at her daily labour a-reaping of her rushes green.

2. I stood, and looked all round me, no other one there could I see,
But me, and my love Mary, I embraced her most tenderly.
She says, "Young man, be easy, don't tease me, but let me be,
Don't you toss my rushes carelessly, great labour they have been to me."

3. "If I toss your rushes carelessly, it's more than I intend to do,
If I toss your rushes carelessly, a bonny bunch I'll reap for you.
Come, and sit you down beside me, although you have led me astray,
Come sit down beside me, for the dew has scarce all gone away."

4. So me, and my love Mary sat down under a laurel tree,
Where the small birds sat in chorus their notes were in high harmony.
The thrush he joined in chorus while I embraced my Arabian queen.
"It's you, I mean, my Mary, and your bonny bunch of rushes green."

5. They kissed, shook hands, and parted although they were to meet again,
To join their hands in wedlock bands, and nevermore to part again.
It's now they have got married, they're out of sorrow, grief, and pain,
And he enjoys his Mary, and her bonny bunch of rushes green.

The Foggy Dew

The Plains of Waterloo

2. I stepped up to this fair one, and says, "My fond creature,
Dare I make so bold as to ask your lover's name?
For I have been in battle where cannons around do rattle,
And by your description I might have known the same."
"Willie Smith's my true love's name, he's a hero of great fame,
He's gone, and he's left me in sorrow, it's true.
No one shall me enjoy but my own darling boy,
And yet he's not returning from the plains of Waterloo."

3. "If Willie Smith's your true love's name, he's a hero of great fame,
He and I have been in battle through manys a long campaign.
Through Italy, and Russia, through Germany, and Prussia,
He was my loyal comrade through France, and through Spain.
Until, at length, by the French, oh, that we were surrounded,
Like heros of old, oh we did them subdue.

4. Oh, the 18th day of June, it ended the battle,
And left manys a fine hero to sigh, and to moan.
The war drums did beat, and the cannons loud did rattle,
'Twas by a French soldier, your Willie he was slain,
And as I passed by where he lay a-bleeding,
I scarcely had time to bid him adieu.
With a faltering voice, of those words he was repeating,
"Farewell, my lovely Annie, you are far from Waterloo."

5. Oh, when this lovely maid heard this sad acclamation,
Her two rosy cheeks they grew pale into one.
When I saw this handsome maid in such lamentation,
I says, "My lovely Annie, I am the very one.
And here is the ring which between us was broken,
In the midst of all dangers to remind me of you."
And when she saw the token, she flew into my arms,
Saying, "My one, and only love, you have returned to me."

The Baskatong

2. We had a foreman, Kennedy was his name,
To speak bad about him would be a great shame.
For suckholes with him, they had no great sight,
For he treated all men in the shanty alike.
chorus

3. Old Kennedy's Dan, he was jovial and true,
He drove a pair of colts there, about twenty-two.
He'd drive fast all day, and he'd never be late,
But he thought he'd play hell if Big Jack had a mate.
chorus

4. Old Kennedy's Dan soon gave them a stroke,
For the very next morning the harness he broke.
He took them to shanty, you may understand,
And told the old man they were just second hand.
chorus

5. Oh, we had a good leader, Morrisette was his name,
To speak bad about him would be a great shame.
He'd lift like a brute when the logs would be large,
Saying, "Up with them boys! Now lift, Joe LeBarge."
chorus

6. Oh, one night we had a great talk
About the herring, that taste of the salt.
And the door of our shanty would give you a fright,
For we're running up and down to the river all night.
chorus

7. I think I'll conclude and finish my song,
I hope you won't mind me for keeping you so long.
But I'll write to my Kate, "Sure it won't be so long,
'Til I'll be returning from the Baskatong."
chorus

The Crúiscín lán*

2. So fill your glasses high, let's not part with lips that's dry,
Though the lark, he proclaims that it is morn.
And if you can't remain, may we shortly meet again,
To have another crúis-cín lán, lán, lán,
For to have another crúis-cín lán.

3. And when grim death appears, after few but pleasant years,
And tells me my race is run.
I'll say, "Begone you slave, great Bacchus gave me leave,
To have another crúis-cín lán, lán, lán,
To have another crúis-cín lán."

*crúiscín lán: (pronounced "Kroosh-keen lawn") Celtic meaning full, small jug.
Edith Fowke's spelling for this Celtic term was "Cruiskeen Lawn".

The Golden Vanity

2. The first came on board was the little cabin boy,
Saying, "Captain what'll you give me if the ship I do destroy?"
"Gold I will give you and my daughter for a bride,
If you sink her in the lowlands, lowlands, lowlands,
If you sink her in the lowlands, low."

3. This boy took an auger and overboard went he,
This boy bent his breast as he swam the raging sea.
He swam 'til he came to the Golden Vanity,
For to sink her in the lowlands, lowlands, lowlands,
For to sink her in the lowlands, low.

4. This boy bored three holes, he bored three holes twice,
While some were playing cards and others shaking dice.
To see their dark eyes twinkle as the water came pouring in,
And them sinking in the lowlands, lowlands, lowlands,
And them sinking in the lowlands, low.

5. This boy turned around and he swam back again,
He swam 'til he came to the Golden Vanity.
Saying, "Captain, pick me up for I'm going with the sea,
And I'm sinking in the lowlands, lowlands, lowlands,
And I'm sinking in the lowlands, low."

6. "Pick you up," said the captain, "that I never will,
Kill you or drown you, I do it with a will.
Gold I will not give you nor my daughter for a bride,
And I'll sink you in the lowlands, lowlands, lowlands
And I'll sink you in the lowlands low."

7. His shipmates picked him up, and 'twas on the deck he died,
They rolled him in a hammock for it was both long and wide.
They rolled him in a hammock and they buried him with the tide,
And he sank in the lowlands, lowlands, lowlands,
And he sank in the lowlands, low.

8. Three weeks thereafter the sun shone bright and clear,
A voice from the heavens, it smote the captain's ear.
Saying, "Captain, cruel Captain, you've been cruel unto me,
And I'll sink you in the lowlands, lowlands, lowlands,
And I'll sink you in the lowlands, low."

9. The captain was amazed, he didn't know what to say,
The captain was amazed as the mainmast gave away.
She levelled with the water, and she sank into the sea,
And she sank in the lowlands, lowlands, lowlands,
And she sank in the lowlands, low.

Finnigan's Wake

Tim Finnigan lived on Walk-er Street, a gen-tle-man I-rish migh-ty odd,
A beauti-ful brogue so rich and sweet and to rise in the world he carried a hod.
But Tim-o-thy had a tip-plin' way with a love of whisk-ey he was born,
And to help him with his work each day a sup of the crath-er took each morn.
chorus
Why car-ay, fa-la-la-da, while the fore your throth-er shake,
Faith it is the truth I told, it's lots of fun at Fin-ni-gan's wake.

2. One morning Tim felt rather full, his head felt heavy which made him shake,
He fell from a ladder, and broke his skull, then they carried him home his corpse to wake.
They rolled him up in a clean sheet and laid him out upon the bed,
With fourteen candles at his feet, and a barrel of whiskey at his head.
chorus

3. His friends assembled at the wake, Mrs. Finnigan called for the lunch,
First they brought in tea and cake, then pipes, and tobacco, and whiskey punch.
Then Judy O'Brien began to cry, "Such a pretty corpse did ever you see,
Ah, Tim, mavourneen, why did you die?" "Shut you mouth," says Judy McGee.
chorus

4. Then Judy O'Brien took up the job, "Now," says she, "you're wrong, I'm sure."
And Judy she hit her a belt in the gob and it sent her sprawling on the floor.
Both sides of the war did soon engage, 'twas woman to woman, and man to man,
Shillelagh law was all the rage, and a bloody surrection soon began.
chorus

5. And Mike Mulvany he ducked his head as a gallon of whiskey flew at him,
It missed him and went onto the bed, and the whiskey scattered over Tim.
Be dad, it revived him, see how he raises, and Timothy jumped up from the bed,
And as they leathered him on both sides, "Bad luck to yourselves, do you think I'm dead?"
chorus

Kelly the Pirate

2. On the 18th of January, so clear was the sky,
When a man on the mainmast so loudly did cry.
When a man of the mainmast so loudly did cry,
"There's a ship in full view and she seems to lay nigh."
Chorus

3. Up stepped our jolly captain, took out his spy glass,
Gave it to the left'nan to see who she was.
He viewed her all over and he viewed her all round,
"It's Kelly the Pirate, I'll bet sixty pounds."
Chorus

4. Four hours sailing brought us within shot
Of the saucy old pirate who valued us not.
Kelly's voice roared like thunder, to his men he did say,
"Place your guns in the hatches and brave boys fire away."
Chorus

5. Four hours broadside and four hours we lay,
While the wads from our guns to his mainmast did fly.
With great shot and mantle Kelly's sides we did wool,
'Til down came his colours, his mainmast and all.
Chorus

6. Now for to conclude and to finish my song,
Here's to that stout frigate that ne'er shall go wrong.
Here's to that stout frigate, that ship of great fame,
That conquered the pirate, George Kelly by name.
Chorus

Song Analysis

	Title	Metre	Toneset/scale	Range
1.	The Sailor's Bride	3/4	major hexachord	1 - 8
2.	The Bold and Undaunted Youth	3/4	major	V - 5
3.	Tread on the Tail of Me Coat	6/8	major	V - 5
4.	Erin Go Bragh	6/8	major	V - 6
5.	Johnny Gallagher	6/8	major	V - 8
6.	Chapeau Boys	6/8	major + ta	1 - 8
7.	The False Young Man	4/4	do pentatonic	VI - 6
8.	Near the Shannon Side	2/4	do pentatonic	V - 6
9.	A Young Man Lived in Belfast Town	2/4	major hexachord	V - 5
10.	The Lovely Banks of Boyne	2/4	major hexachord	1 - 8
11.	The Keyhole in the Door	2/4	major hexachord	1 - 9
12.	Down by Yon Shady Harbour	2/4	major hexachord	1 - 9
13.	The Dog and His Gun	2/4	major hexachord	1 - 10
14.	Erin's Lovely Home I	2/4	incomplete major	1 - 10
15.	Erin's Lovely Home II	2/4	major hexachord	1 - 10
16.	There Was an Old Woman	2/4	incomplete major	III - 5
17.	By Borden's Grove	2/4	incomplete major	V - 8
18.	The Banks of Sweet Dundee	2/4	major	1 - 8
19.	My Good Looking Man	2/4	major	1 - 10
20.	The Maid of Sweet Gurteen	2/4	incomplete mixolydian	1 - 8
21.	The Gypsy Daisy	2/4	mixolydian	1 - 8
22.	The Mower	2/4	mixolydian	1 - 9
23.	The Farmer's Son and the Shantyboy	2/4	mixolydian	III - 5
24.	Skibbereen	2/4	incomplete aeolian	VII - 8
25.	By the Rosy Banks So Green	2/4	dorian	VII - 8
26.	The Hat My Father Wore	2/4	dorian	1 - ♭10
27.	The Lass of Glenshee	3/4	la pentatonic	1 - 8
28.	On the Banks of the Don	3/4	do pentatonic	V - 6
29.	Lost Jimmy Whelan	3/4	dorian	V - 5
30.	As I Roved through an Irish Town	3/4	major hexachord	V - 4
31.	I'll Write You a Letter	3/4	major hexachord	V - 6
32.	Tommy and the Apple	3/4	major	VII - 8
33.	Pat O'Donnell	6/8	la pentatonic	1 - ♭10
34.	The Colleen Bawn	6/8	do pentatonic	VI - 8

35.	The Dying Girl	6/8	incomplete aeolian	IV - 5
36.	Barney Blake	6/8	major hexachord	1 - 10
37.	My Charming Sally Ann	6/8	major hexachord	1 - 8
38.	The Barley Grain for Me	6/8	major	V - 5
39.	Cooper and Donnelly	6/8	major	1 - 8
40.	A Bunch of Watercresses	6/8	major	III - 4
41.	The Lonesome Scenes of Winter	6/8	major	III - 6
42.	The Drunkard's Dream	6/8	major	V - 6
43.	Home, Green Erin, O	6/8	major	1 - 9
44.	My Bonny Irish Boy	6/8	incomplete mixolydian +ta	1 - 8
45.	The Green Linnet	6/8	major hexachord	1 - 8
46.	Daniel O'Connell	6/8	major hexachord	1 -10
47.	A Man You Don't Meet Every Day	6/8	major	1 - 8
48.	Over the Mountain	6/8	major	#VII - 8
49.	The Blackwater Side	6/8	major	1 - 9
50.	The Banks of the Dee	6/8	mixolydian	V - 7
51.	The Black Bottle	6/8	major + ta	I - 4
52.	Terrence's Farewell	6/8	incomplete aeolian	V - 8
53.	Old Erin	6/8	la pentachord/ mixolydian	VII - 8
54.	The Farmer's Boy	4/4	major hexachord	V - 6
55.	Captain Colstein	4/4	major	V - 6
56.	The Banks of Newfoundland	4/4	major	1 - 9
57.	By the Hush, Me Boys	4/4	mixolydian	VII - 8
58.	The Soldier's Farewell	4/4	mixolydian	III - 6
59.	The Bonny Bunch of Rushes Green	4/4	mixolydian + fi	V - 7
60.	The Foggy Dew	4/4	la pentatonic + ti	VII - 9
61.	The Plains of Waterloo	4/4	dorian	1 - ♭10
62.	The Baskatong	6/8	major	1 - 8
63.	The Crúiscín lán	2/4	aeolian	V - 8
64.	The Golden Vanity	2/4	major	II - 4
65.	Finnigan's Wake	2/4	major hexachord	V - 6
66.	Kelly the Pirate	3/4	incomplete aeolian	V - 5

Tonesets/Scales

la pentatonic	27, 33
la pentatonic + ti	60
la pentatonic/mixolydian	53
do pentatonic	7, 8, 28, 34
major hexachord	1, 9, 10, 11, 12, 13, 15, 30, 31, 36, 37, 45, 46, 54, 65
incomplete major	14, 16, 17
incomplete aeolian	24, 35, 52, 66
incomplete mixolydian	20
major	2, 3, 4, 5, 18, 19, 32, 38, 39, 40, 41, 42, 43, 47, 48, 49, 55, 56, 62, 64
aeolian	63
dorian	25, 26, 29, 61
mixolydian	21, 22, 23, 50, 57, 58, 62, 64
major + ta	6, 51
incomplete mixolydian + ta	44
mixolydian + fi	59

Ranges

seven	V - 4	30
octave	V - 5	2, 3, 9, 29, 38, 66
	VI - 6	7
	1 - 8	1, 6, 10, 18, 20, 21, 27, 37, 39, 44, 45, 47, 62
nine	III - 4	40
	IV - 5	35
	V - 6	4, 8, 28, 31, 42, 54, 55, 65
	VII - 8	24, 25, 32, 53, 57
	#VII - 8	48
	1 - 9	11, 12, 22, 43, 49, 56
ten	II - 4	64
	III - 5	16, 23
	V - 7	50, 59
	VI - 8	34
	VII - 9	60
	1 - ♭10	26, 33, 61
	1 - 10	13, 14, 15, 19, 36, 46
eleven	I - 4	51
	III - 6	41, 58
	V - 8	5, 17, 52, 63

Edith Fowke

Edith Fulton Fowke was an avid proponent of folklore, folk music, and folk singers. Born in 1913 in Lumsden, Saskatchewan, Edith Fulton earned a master's degree in English literature at the University of Saskatchewan (1937). In 1938 she married Frank Fowke, whom she had met at university, and moved to Toronto. They had been married for fifty-eight years when Edith died in 1996.

In Saskatchewan, and later in Ontario, she and Frank were influenced by J. S. Woodsworth, Tommy Douglas, and others in the socialist movement of the Co-operative Commonwealth Federation (CCF), which later became the New Democratic Party (NDP). This interest in the "common folk" led quite naturally to an interest in folklore, and folk song. By the 1950s the Fowkes had quite a large collection of folk song recordings. Edith convinced Harry Boyle, Program Director at the Canadian Broadcasting Corporation (CBC) to let her try a weekly program, Folk Song Time, using her recordings interspersed with narrative. Each week she had a different theme: sailor songs, lumbering songs, songs about disasters, love songs, and so on. This program continued, with some interruptions, until 1964.

In the meantime, Edith and Canadian composer and academic, Richard Johnston, teamed up to publish Folk Songs of Canada (1954), Folk Songs of Québec (1957), and More Folk Songs of Canada (1967). In preparing Folk Songs of Canada, Edith observed that there were very few published songs from west of Québec and particularly few from Ontario. This sparked a curiosity in collecting which was heightened by a visit to the eminent folk music researcher, Helen Creighton, in Nova Scotia in 1953. Influenced by this visit, and a subsequent visit to Kenneth Goldstein, a folk music collector in the United States, she purchased a tape recorder in order to begin collecting. The interview with Frank Fowke describes some of their early collecting trips in the Peterborough area.

One singer led to another, and so her collection began. She found O. J. Abbott through his daughter, who wrote to say that her father had a large repertoire of songs. In a paper titled "My Life in Canadian Folksong Research," given in 1988 at the First Conference on Ethnomusicology in Canada, Edith Fowke says of O. J. Abbott, "He was undoubtedly the prize of my collection."[4]

One observation Edith Fowke made was that Irish songs dominated Canadian folk music, not only in Newfoundland, but all across the country. Another observation was that she was able to collect more songs from Catholics than from Protestants. Edith speculated that perhaps Protestants were supposed to sing in praise of God, whereas Catholics were allowed to sing secular songs.[5]

Edith Fowke attended many folk festivals in Canada, the United States, and Great Britain. She became a personal friend of many of the singers. In this way she was able to hear and to discover more variants of songs, as well as to make historical connections between songs heard in North America and their older roots in Britain.

Because she was not a trained musician, Edith Fowke could not transcribe her own songs and had to rely on others for this meticulous task. In a letter to Peggy Seeger, dated August 29, 1963, Edith says,

> I'm judging from texts more than tunes: I don't trust my judgment on tunes because I tend to rate a poor tune sung by a good singer better than a good tune sung by a poor singer.[6]

She goes on to say,

> I've drawn heavily on Mr. Abbott – partly because he sang so many songs and also because his texts are unusually good. However, I may be overestimating the value of his tunes because I like the way he sings them.

Several renowned musicians, including Alan Mills, Peggy Seeger, Keith MacMillan, Jay Rahn, and others, transcribed the songs for her various publications.

Edith held a strong conviction that people should hear songs as sung by her singers rather than simply seeing them in print. Her next project was a series of books and recordings from her Ontario collection. During her travels in the United States she made a connection with Folkways Records. They produced a number of recordings from her collection including Irish and British Songs from the Ottawa Valley sung by O. J. Abbott (1961), Lumbering Songs from the Ontario Shanties (1961) and Songs of the Great Lakes (1964). Later, Edith brought out two recordings in England, one of songs sung by LaRena Clark on Topic records (1965) and the other, Far Canadian Fields, on Leader (1975).

Other printed collections followed: Canada's Story in Song (1965), Traditional Singers and Songs from Ontario (1965), Lumbering Songs from the Northern Woods (1970), Penguin Book of Canadian Folk Songs (1973), and Singing Our History (1984).

Edith became interested in children's lore and began collecting songs and singing games in her own neighbourhood, and then in a number of schools in Toronto. Sally Go Round the Sun (1969) and Ring Around the Moon (1977) include songs, singing and clapping games, ball-bouncing chants, and rhymes. These two books, as well as Folk Songs of Canada and the Penguin Book of Canadian Folk Songs, are well known to many elementary school teachers in Canada.

In the article in Ethnomusicology in Canada (1990), Edith says that after 1973 she felt she had published enough books about folk songs and was ready to turn her attention more to folklore. She continued to write articles and to teach. In 1971, Edith Fowke began to teach at York University, where she lectured for thirteen years. When she retired in 1984, she was made a professor emeritus. Edith Fowke received honorary degrees from Brock, Trent, and Regina universities and was appointed a Member of the Order of Canada. She died on March 28, 1996, a month short of her 83rd birthday.

O. J. Abbott

Oliver John Abbott (1872–1962) was born in England but immigrated to Canada with his brother, Walter, when he was twelve and Walter was about sixteen. Bernard Abbott, son of O. J. Abbott, says that the family knows very little about why the two boys were sent to Canada by themselves at such a young age. Apparently, their mother was an actress, probably alone, and unable to support two young boys. Unfortunately, Walter fell off a hay wagon and was killed when he was still quite young.[7]

O. J., as he was always known, and Walter lived in the Ottawa Valley with the Whalen family and later with the O'Malley's. The Whalen's were a particularly musical family and many of the songs O. J. Abbott sang were ones he had learned in this home as a teenager and a young man. The Whalen family, and the community of South March (eight miles south of Ottawa) in which they lived, was largely of Irish descent, and therefore there was a predominance of songs from the Irish heritage. The songs they sang had been brought from Ireland by their grandparents. O. J. Abbott learned many of his songs from Mrs. Whalen and Mrs. O'Malley.

In the late 1800s the young men in the Ottawa Valley would traditionally work on the farms in the summer and hire out to the logging camps in the winter. The older boys that O. J. Abbott knew as a youth brought new songs home from the camps with them each year. Even before he was old enough to work in the camps himself, O. J. had a significant collection of songs learned from the local families and from the older boys with whom he worked on the farms.

When he was about twenty he began to work in the camps. The first winter he worked for J. R. Booth Co. at South River, Lake Nippissing, the second in Ostabanna for Buel and Hurdman, and the third for Camble and Gibson on the French River, Algoma District. Later he worked near Mattawa on the Mab-de-feaux for Mackey Sons and Co.

Evenings, both on the farms and in the camps, were frequently spent singing songs. In a paper titled "History of English Ballads Research in Ontario," Edith Fowke writes, referring to the dominant influence of the lumber camps,

> The shantyboys created the largest body of native songs, and played a major role in preserving, and spreading songs of all kinds in this province. Men went to work in the lumberwoods in the fall, and in the long winter months before radio and television they had to make their own entertainment. They sang all the songs they knew, and learned those known by other men who came from

different areas. When they came home in the spring they passed on their enlarged repertoire to others in their communities.[8]

Although many of the songs were Anglo/Celtic in origin, some were original, and some migrated north from the United States. O. J. Abbott also sang a number of sea shanties, which seem to have come from Cape Breton and must have been sung in the camps as well.

In his twenties O. J. Abbott married and moved to Hull, Québec, where he lived for the rest of his life. He worked for the Canadian Pacific Railway from 1900 to 1904, the Canadian Cement Co. until 1908, and then as an oiler for thirty-nine years with J. R. Booth Paper Mill (later E. B. Eddy), after which he retired. Twelve children were born to this family, six of whom survived into adulthood.

As part of her CBC program, Folk Song Time, Edith Fowke played songs that she and others had collected. Mrs. Ida Dagenais of Saskatchewan heard one such program and wrote to tell Edith that her father who lived in Hull had a large repertoire of songs and asked her if she was interested. Edith wrote back to ask for a list of some of the songs. She found that there were some that she already knew, but many that she didn't. In the liner notes to the recording, Irish and British Songs from the Ottawa Valley, Edith describes her meeting with O. J. Abbott.

> The most exciting adventure of my collecting so far was the discovery of Mr. O. J. Abbott of Hull, Québec. Mr. Abbott, now eighty-five, is the finest traditional singer I've had the pleasure of meeting, and I don't expect to come across many more like him. He knows well over a hundred folk songs, and he recorded eighty-four of them for me in 1957.[9]

She goes on to say:

> Mr. Abbott turned out to be a short, chubby man with white hair and sparkling eyes. In view of his age, I hardly expected he'd be able to sing very well, but I hoped the tapes would be good enough to preserve the words, and give some idea of the tunes. Imagine my delight when I started the tape recorder, and he began to sing in a fresh, clear voice, full of character, and right on pitch.... His songs were mostly complete and well-rounded, and as he swung into each new song, his style and rhythm changed to express the new mood. He is a natural born singer, and he seems to have perfect "phonographic" memory, for he could reproduce, almost instantly, songs he had not sung for fifty to sixty years.[10]

It is clear that O. J. Abbott was not only one of Edith Fowke's most prolific singers, but also a favourite. She featured his recordings many times on Folk Song Time between 1957 and 1964. In 1958, Edith had O. J. Abbott sing at the National Museum in Ottawa during a lecture she was giving on Ontario folk songs. The following year Pete

Seeger invited him to sing a few songs in an Ottawa concert. In 1960, he appeared on CBC television with Pete Seeger at the Newport Folk Festival. In 1961, he sang at the Mariposa Folk Festival in Orillia and at the International Folk Music Council in Québec City. He died in March, 1962, at the venerable age of ninety.

Interview with Frank Fowke

JP: Would you please tell me how you met Edith, and how she got started in folk music collecting?

FF: Well, I met Edith when I went to the Saskatchewan University to take first-year engineering. They had a get-acquainted dance to start off the social activities. So I went to the dance, and danced with her a few times, and later took her out to a show, and kept in touch with her through the year. She never encouraged me very much. We'd have a date to go to a show. I'd arrive on time, and she'd be twenty minutes late, and have an excuse that she was helping somebody with some work they had to do. In the four years before we got married, we were only together the one year. The second year she was out teaching, and the third year she was back in Saskatoon. I went to Winnipeg for fourth-year electrical engineering, and the next year I was teaching in a school forty or fifty miles outside of Saskatoon. I managed to see her once or twice that year. So we didn't keep in very close contact. When I decided to come to Ontario – this was in 1937 – in the Depression, I was lucky enough to get a job in engineering, and I've been here ever since. We got married after I'd been down here for a year. That's how she came to come to Toronto.

JP: What got her interested in folklore and folk music collecting?

FF: It was a gradual process. We got a record player during the war, and we found that we were buying all the records of folksongs that were available at that time. There weren't many. During the war Edith worked for a magazine called The Magazine Digest that was published in Toronto. It was very much like the Reader's Digest. During the war they had good sales because they were exporting most of their production to the States. Reader's Digest couldn't get paper to print their magazine. But when the war was over, and Reader's Digest got back into the market again, the Magazine Digest just folded up, and Edith was out of a job. She got the idea of putting on a radio program of folksongs because we had a fairly large collection by that time. She went down, and sold the idea to somebody at the CBC. They tried her out with a couple of three-month contracts to start with, and finally it was all year round – an hour's program every Saturday. By that time more records were available on the market.

JP: At this point had she done any collecting herself?

FF: No, she hadn't. It was about 1953 when we went to Nova Scotia on a holiday, and looked up Helen Creighton. We'd seen Helen Creighton's book, you know, and Roy Mackenzie was another one who collected in Nova Scotia. We found Helen Creighton out along the coast somewhere getting songs from the fishermen, and she had a tape recorder. This was when the first tape recorders were available. Helen Creighton did most of her collecting with a pencil and a pad of notepaper, writing the words down, and to get the tune she had an instrument that was a cross between an accordion, and a reed organ. She could carry this with her in a wheelbarrow, and she'd play the tune on this until she got it so the singer said it was right, and then she could write it down in musical notation. With a tape recorder all this is unnecessary. By this time Edith was thinking about doing some collecting so in the fall she visited Ken Goldstein in Philadelphia, and came back with a tape recorder.

Later that fall, she decided to try some collecting. We tried a couple of other places but she was pretty sure that Peterborough would be the best place to collect songs. She thought we'd get more songs from Catholics than Protestants because John Knox and John Calvin frowned on singing folksongs. They thought singing should be to praise the Lord.

We knew a man who worked in the office of the local newspaper in Peterborough, but he couldn't help us any so we went to the local priest. We told him what we wanted. He put his head down, and gave us a long, hard look over the top of his glasses. I guess he decided that we were genuine, or at least harmless, so he gave us the names of several people who he thought could help us. One of them was a Mrs. Town who ran a general store in a town not far from Peterborough, and she was a big help to us. Anyway, we'd go to one of these people, and ask them if they knew any of the lumber camp songs. That's the way we identified what we wanted.

Almost the first person we went to knew what kind of songs we were talking about, but he didn't sing them himself. But he said, "The man you want to see is my uncle, Martin Sullivan. He used to work in the lumber camps, and he knows all those old songs."

We said, "That's exactly the kind of man we're looking for. Where does he live?"

He couldn't tell us, or didn't want to tell us. Anyway, we went on collecting from other people because nearly always when we got a song from one person, they'd tell us about somebody else, and we'd get different songs from them. Several of them mentioned Martin Sullivan, but nobody could tell us where he lived. Finally, it was Mrs. Town that solved the problem for us. When we asked her about Martin Sullivan she said, "Oh, I can tell you where to find Martin Sullivan. He's in the Peterborough Jail." It wasn't as bad as it sounded. He hadn't committed a serious crime, or any crime at all. He was in his late fifties when we knew him, and he just made a living by working as a farm labourer. He'd get a job with a farmer in the spring and stay with him through seeding, and haying, and harvest, and thrashing, and so on, right though the year. He was a good worker as long as he stayed sober, but he was a helpless alcoholic. His employer would know what his problem was and take steps to keep things under control. Marty would always want to go into Peterborough on Saturday night, and have a few drinks. So his employer would pay him some of his wages, enough for a few drinks, but not enough to go on a real binge. He'd come back Sunday afternoon, and be ready for work Monday morning.

It went on this way until late in the fall when the fall work was all done, and his employer didn't need him any longer, so he'd pay him the rest of his wages. Martin would go into Peterborough, and instead of putting some money in the bank for safekeeping, and finding a good boarding place for the winter, he'd start drinking. He wouldn't be sober until his money was all gone. The police would find him sleeping on a park bench or on somebody's front lawn. They'd charge him with vagrancy, and throw him in the slammer. At the next session of court, they'd bring him before the justice of the peace or whoever was acting as judge, and the judge would recognize him. This happened every year.

The judge would say, "Oh, good day, Mr. Sullivan. Are you here again? What's the charge this time?"

So the clerk of the court would read out the charge. The judge would say, "Oh, vagrancy. Same old thing."

The policeman would look up his notes, and say where they found him, and under what conditions, and the judge would say, "How do you plead, Mr. Sullivan? Are you innocent or guilty?"

He'd say, "Guilty, Your Honour."

And the judge would say, "You don't have a lawyer. Do you have anything to say in your own defence?" But he wouldn't even try to defend himself, you know.

So the judge would say, "Well, Mr. Sullivan, my job is to try to persuade you to change your ways. I haven't had much luck so far, but I'm going to be pretty severe with you this time." And he'd sentence him to about three months in jail. This would be the best thing that could happen to him. He'd have a roof over his head, and three meals a day, and no alcohol. He'd while away his time through the winter, and get out about the end of February. The farmers would hire him, and the saga would start all over again.

JP: So did you go to the jail to get the songs from him?

FF: No, we contacted him the next summer when he was working again. We went out to this farm Sunday afternoon, and along about four o'clock he came walking down the road. He was quite pleased to sing for us. The songs he knew weren't new to us but sometimes it was a different version. I had to go along to carry the tape recorder. It weighed about forty pounds. Edith couldn't even lift it off the floor so I had to carry it around.

JP: Did you go on most of the trips?

FF: Well, for a while. After that Edith got a lighter tape recorder that she could manage herself. Then she collected quite on her own.

JP: Tell me about meeting O. J. Abbott.

FF: I was just going to say that one singer would tell us of another singer. And we kept going that way. When Edith had her program Folk Song Time on the air, it was a one-hour program on Saturday afternoon about one o'clock. She got a letter from a woman from Swift Current, Saskatchewan, who was a nurse, and was nursing in a hospital out there. She told Edith about her father who lived in Hull, Quebec. She said he knew a lot of the old songs, and she should meet him and get some of his songs. That summer we took my two-week holiday and went up to Ottawa and Hull to look up O. J. Abbott. He was quite willing to sing for us. He was about eighty-five at that time, but he had a good strong voice, and he sang in tune. One thing about the singers is that they always sang unaccompanied. When they started a song they'd stop and think for a minute to get the pitch right and the first few words, then they'd start right off, right on the tune, and sing it right through.

JP: What we noticed on the tapes of O. J. Abbott songs was that in the first verse he'd be a little unsure of the melody, but by the second verse he was a little stronger, and a little better, and the melody was more accurate.

FF: I think we spent two afternoons with him, maybe more than that, and when the number of songs got up to around seventy or eighty he said, "Well, I'll give you a song for every year of my age." And he did. Edith went back a couple of times after that, and he gave her some more songs. I think it was about 120 songs she got from him altogether.

JP: Yes, I'm not sure, but it's a lot. Many of them have multiple verses.

FF: Some of them are quite long. One of the singers told us that he got a lot of the songs in the lumber camps. The reason the songs were spread around so much was that to entertain themselves in the evening they sang unaccompanied – that was about all they had to do. They didn't even have an instrument. Those who could learn a song and sing it would learn all the songs they could in that camp. The next year they'd probably be in a different camp, and take their songs to that camp. So the songs were spread around.

JP: There would probably be a little different variant in each camp. By the time you took it to the next camp you might have changed a few things.

FF: This chap told us he just had to hear a song once, and he could remember it. He said when he heard a song he wanted to remember he'd go to his bunk so there wouldn't be any interference and sing it over in his head. If there was a line he couldn't remember, he'd make up a line of his own which fitted the song, and that was how we got variations, I guess.

When Edith got a lighter tape recorder that she could carry around by herself she often went out on her own, and I didn't know so much about the later collecting. There was one chap we got a few songs from, but they were songs we didn't get from anybody else. Something happened to the tape, and Edith decided she wanted to tape them over again. Edith wrote him a note, and said we'd be up to see him. When we got to the door his wife met us, and she was full of apologies. She was sorry he wasn't there. He'd been there half an hour ago. He knew we were coming, but he'd gone into town, and she didn't know when he'd be back. She didn't think there was any use waiting. This happened twice, and we were kind of puzzled, wondering if we'd done something to offend him. Edith mentioned this to Mrs. Town, and she said she knew what was the matter. He'd been drinking too much. But she had an idea. Lent was coming soon, and he always went on the wagon for Lent. So about the second weekend in Lent we went up. Edith had written him a note, and he was waiting for us. When we drove in he came out, greeted us warmly and invited us into the house. He was in good voice. He sang his songs, and Edith recorded them. Everything was fine.

Frank Fowke, 1996
Personal Interview
Toronto, Ontario

Interview with Richard Johnson

JP: Dr. Johnson, would you please tell me about your connection with Edith Fowke? I know that you published several books together.

RJ: She was a many-faceted gem. We met through a student in my second year [as a professor] at the University of Toronto. She was not a musician, but she claimed she had enough material to publish a book of folksongs. Was I interested in working with her?

Before I came to Canada I became interested in folk songs because some of our relatives from Sweden moved to Chicago where we lived. I remember we used to sing Swedish folk songs, and have Swedish dancing in our basement.

My students understood that I had a kind of interest in folk music since I used Bach chorales, based on folk tunes, in my theory classes. While I hadn't yet evinced an interest in Canadian folk music, along came Edith Fowke, and I was hooked.

Edith was one of those people who had a focus. She was convinced that she could make a very real impact as an authority on Canadian folk music, and she certainly proved it. Later on, when I met her husband, Frank, I learned that he was not interested in folk songs as much as in folk dancing, but he was a very big helpmate to Edith.

JP: Did he go on her collecting trips?

RJ: He went on some of her collecting trips with her, but, as well, he kept her papers, and recordings organized. She had a huge record collection of 78's. These are really valuable now because there is so much material there that hasn't been re-recorded.

As I mentioned, this student brought Edith and me together, but there was no question of whether or not we would work together. Edith had decided that that was what was going to happen, and when she decided something, it was impossible to break her away from even a detail. I tried many times! While Edith didn't know, and, as far as I know, didn't ever learn one thing about one note of music, she could recognize a tune. She couldn't sing, or at least, she didn't ever sing for me.

She was anxious to make contact with Marius Barbeau in Ottawa. She and I hopped in my car, and went to Ottawa for a weekend, and spent a very, very wonderful time with Barbeau. That happened two or three times. Later on, I got to know Barbeau very well, and that's when he and I organized, or I should say reorganized, the Canadian Folk Music Society. It had existed beforehand, but nothing really had happened. We got it going. Edith was not involved in the organization at that time because it was not about collecting, and she was focused on collecting. She knew what she wanted to do, and nothing stopped her, and that's very good.

JP: What got her started?

RJ: I'm not certain, but, you see, she was a socialist, and so was Frank. They were involved in the CCF [Co-Operative Commonwealth Federation] party, and there were all sorts of clubs sponsored by the CCF. They included folk song clubs, and dancing clubs with very real intelligence behind them. Edith came from Saskatchewan, and Tommy Douglas was very busy in those days involving the farmers in doing what they could do, from a socialist point of view. At that time there was hardly a Canadian-born person in Saskatchewan. They were all Swedes and Norwegians, Germans, Poles, Bohemians, Ukrainians. They all had their little cliques, and they all had their own newspapers in their own languages. The thing that brought them together was folk music. Tommy Douglas was the guy who knew this. Edith got the bug then. When she and Frank moved to Toronto she maintained her political interests. They were expressed through folklore. That's how she got started.

At first Edith knew all of the books. She was always a book person. She had a university degree. Edith was an extraordinarily bright woman – a member of Mensa. She had a huge library of this material [folksong and folklore books]. It was all over the place and she wanted to bring it together. In those days, remember, [mid-1940s, 1950s] there were all sorts of folk singers on CBC too, such as Alan Mills, Burl Ives, and Pete Seeger. These were all great friends of Edith's. There were all sorts of folk clubs in Toronto. I came to Toronto in 1947, and I met her in the fall of 1948, and we got going.

JP: When was your first publication with her? When did Folk Songs of Canada come out first?

RJ: I think it was 1949 or 1950, something like that [The actual publication date is 1954.], and that was interesting too because she said, "Let's do a book," and so I said, "Who's the publisher?" and she said, "I don't know, do you?"

I came to Canada in the second year of the Music Education program at the University of Toronto under Sir Ernest MacMillan. Here we were, I was a professor in this course that was turning out the first university-trained music teachers in Canada, and that was of great interest to many people including C. F. Thiele who was the head of Waterloo Music Company. I got to know him, and when Edith asked who would publish I suggested Waterloo Music. Theile understood the school market as he had been publishing band music already. When I said a book of folk music he said, "With an edition for schools?" He said, "Done" and we were away. I didn't have much of a library of that sort of thing at that time although I started buying pretty fast. Edith had this big library, and she was very generous at sharing the library with me. I knew some of the folksongs common to both countries [Canada and the United States], but I didn't know the specifically Canadian ones. I had to learn these, and it was great chance to learn something about my [new] country.

Well, that's how Edith and I got going, and we had pitched battles. We fought tooth and nail about details of every kind. I had the upper hand when it came to publication because she didn't know the publisher and I did, and I was the musician. My wife [Canadian pianist Yvonne Johnston] knew someone who was the right person

[Elizabeth Hoey] to do the illustrations for the first book. Edith was interested in the political, social, and historical end of folk music, and she did a magnificent job.

JP: Are songs that Edith collected in Folk Songs of Canada?

RJ: No, most of those songs are from other collections. For example, there used to be a weekly newspaper in Saskatchewan that published a song collected from somebody in Saskatchewan in every issue. This was naturally a source for our work. Then, there were all of the people like Alan Mills singing on the radio and making recordings. I transcribed some of the songs from those recordings.

JP: When Alan Mills sang was it from printed music or from oral tradition?

RJ: I think it was a little bit of both. He had a big repertoire so I don't think he learned all his songs from informants. There were books in print in those days that had a lot of Canadian material in them. They weren't always recognized as Canadian. It took Edith to correct some of those unintentional errors, and identify some songs as Canadian rather than American.

We did Folk Songs of Canada, solo edition with piano accompaniment, then Folk Songs of Canada choral arrangements for the schools, then More Folk Songs of Canada, then we did Folk Songs of Quebec, which came out in two editions, solo with piano accompaniment and the choral edition.

JP: Did Edith do all the research for materials in these books?

RJ: Oh, yes. I did some, but I was mainly the musician, the arranger. I put the material into presentable form. I was busy teaching so my time was limited, and I was newly married.

For a long time Edith and I barely tolerated each other – we're both strong personalities – but we needed each other. In the later years, though, we became very good friends. I always called her when I went to Toronto and we met someplace or I went out to her house. I think we became genuinely fond of each other. I certainly respect all of the things that she stood for.

Thanks to Mr. Thiele and Fred Moogk [also of Waterloo Music], I was introduced to the Mennonites. I got some songs from a Mennonite who was subsequently shunned by his congregation for three months [because he sang their songs to an outsider]. When Kodály came to Toronto in 1966, we took him to Stratford. Then we took him around the Mennonite Amish communities north of Stratford. I found a place where they were having a Sunday service in a barn, but they would not let us come in. That was sad because Kodály was anxious to see such a service, as were we all. We got there just before the service started. The elders had a little meeting, and then came out and said, "No, we won't allow you in. Please go away." We did visit some of their cemeteries, and that was of great interest to Kodály. I had a couple of Mennonites in my theory classes, and I began collecting from the more modern Mennonites. I told Edith to do the same.

That's when she found La Rena Clark and then O. J. Abbott. She made a big thing out of both of those informants, and rightfully so. Up to that point she hadn't collected anything. But she discovered that she really enjoyed the collecting. Edith was not what you call a social being. She always wanted to be the "Grand Dame" and she was a first-class authority. She knew the history, and she knew the literature. She was a social historian, and a lorist.

JP: Edith had a large collection of Folkways recordings. Were these recordings made from transcribed music or from field tapes?

RJ: You'll have to ask Frank Fowke about that. I'm not sure, but he'll know.

We took some things off of Folkways recordings. Folkways recordings, after all, are American, but singers like Pete Seeger were singing "North American" material, not just strictly U.S. material, and I think that's right.

JP: Many of the songs were trans-border anyway, weren't they?

RJ: Oh, absolutely. But in both cases, in the United States, and in Canada, there is a lot of real source material. Most of the songs, in any case, came originally from Europe. We were far behind the States when it came to transportation and communication. I don't know many Icelandic folksongs because those immigrants lived in Northern Ontario, and Manitoba where communication was limited [in those days].

When we first began to work together I did not know the Canadian material, and I did not have the Canadian published material to work with that Edith had. She had a big, big wonderful library. We'd have a weekly or a bi-weekly meeting to talk about the make-up of the next book. She had lists of material – she made lots of lists. Some of the songs I knew, and some I didn't. She would give me the material. Sometimes we'd have a little bit of a battle. She wanted a particular song because of its social, labour, or historical implications. If it was really bad, junky music I would refuse it, and sometimes we had pretty serious arguments. We fought hard, but I never gave in on the quality of the music side. I think that might be one reason she then went to Penguin, and published the Penguin book [The Penguin Book of Canadian Folksongs]. She was the sole authority there.

She was working with Keith MacMillan for several years at her weekly program. Keith was a very, very good musician, but he never interfered with the taste of the person he was recording. He would simply accept. He was not there to do anything except facilitate the broadcast. So she crammed a lot of stuff onto her radio program that I would have been critical of.

While we had a number of rifts earlier, during the last number of years that she was alive, whenever we met it was with pleasure on both sides. She made a big contribution. I was surprised, and very pleased when I learned that she left her collection to the University of Calgary Library Special Collections. All of my material is in the University of Calgary library, and I'm pleased that they are there together.

Richard Johnston, 1996
Personal Interview

Appendix A: Stories of O. J. Abbott

The following stories were told to Edith Fowke by O. J. Abbott, and recorded along with his songs. The first one paints a picture of one aspect of work in a lumber camp in the Ottawa Valley. The second one tells of curing a toothache by evoking a charm. In transcribing these stories, I have tried to retain the speech patterns of Mr. Abbott, which were quite typical of the Ottawa Valley in the 1950s.

Cutting Square Timbers

As told to Edith Fowke by O. J. Abbott in 1958

O. J.: I worked in a square timber shanty for a while. Of course, there was a liner, and two scorers. They used to cut down the tree, and if there was a punk or anything like that in the tree, they wouldn't use it. They'd just leave the whole tree there. Sometimes they wouldn't even make a log out of it. But that's a long time ago. Well, they'd fell the tree. The liners would line it up, and the scorers would come along, and cut a notch in it, and cut the blocks off. They'd cut the blocks off the side of the tree, and then hack it along. Then the hewer would come, and hew the tree – square it. They'd do one side, then they'd cant the tree over, and make it square then. Of course, a team of horses had to come along to cant it over – it was pretty hard to do it with a cant hook. Then the man would come along with his team of horses, and chain it to a sloop and bring it down to the river, unhitch the chain, draw the sleigh out from under, and let it fall in the river.

E.F.: What year was that?

O. J.: Now, you'd have to go back sixty-five years anyway [late 1880s].

E.F.: And then in the camps where they made them into logs, how did they do that?

O. J.: They just felled the tree, and measured them off, sixteen feet or twelve feet long – whatever the tree would make. Supposing the tree would make three sixteen-foot logs or three twelve-foot logs, they'd cut it off in that. The man would come along with the team of horses, and hitch on a pair of tongs, pull them out, and draw them down to the skidway. There was a man at the skidway to roll them down the skidway, pile them up on the skidway until it was up to the level of the ground. Then they'd have to make another skidway in a different place. When the snow would come, they'd quit making logs and draw them to the river. They had bobsleighs. They'd load them onto the bobsleighs – ten, twelve, fifteen logs, and draw them to the river. There was a man at the river who would unchain them, and let them fall in the river ready for the drive when the ice would go away in the spring.

Glossary

punk: dry, crumbly wood useful for tinder
blocks: hindrance, branches
cant: tilt
hew: to give shape to with an axe
bobsleigh: a short sled usually used as one of a joined pair.
tong: a grasping device
skidway: a timber or rail over or on which something is slid or rolled
Historical note: Square timbers of white pine were in great demand by Britain in the mid-nineteenth century, not only for building houses, but for its massive ship-building industry. The timbers were floated to the Ottawa River in the spring break-up, rafted together and carried down the Ottawa River to the St. Lawrence, and on to Quebec where they were loaded into ocean-going vessels. The industry had pretty well collapsed by 1900.[11]

Curing the Toothache – A Folk Tale

as told to Edith Fowke in 1958

    E.F.: Tell me how to cure a toothache.

    O. J.: Tell you how to cure a toothache. I can't.

    E.F.: But you do it. Tell us how you do it.

    O. J.: I can't. I can't give it away.

    E.F.: Oh, it's a secret? You can't tell me about it?

    O. J.: No, I can't give it away. I worked with a fella named Albert Tapp in the shanty on French River, and I had a toothache. I would've had to go forty mile out to catch the stage to go down to a doctor for to get my tooth cured. I couldn't speak, I couldn't open my mouth hardly. So we were lying on the bunk, and I said, "Well, I guess I've have to go down in the morning, Albert." And when I mentioned that now – there were twenty-seven went up from Ottawa together. We hired for the spring drive. If you go down in the spring they can let you go any time they like. You see. They'll tell a man, "Bring your axe tonight. You're going down tomorrow."

So there was just me, and Albert Tapp, and a fella named Jack Lawrence that they didn't tell us to bring in our axe. There was only the three of us so we stayed for the drive – the three of us. I was just wishing that they wouldn't tell me to bring in me axe anytime.

So he says, "You're staying for the drive."

I said, "Yes, but if I've got to go down now I won't be able to come back for the drive. I'll go ahead to Ottawa."

He says, "You're not going down." So we turned over and went to sleep. After a while he says, "How's your tooth?"

I says, "It's not achin' a bit. Not at all."

He says, "It won't ache no more."

I got up in the morning – my tooth was all right. I worked all that spring on the drive, and come down to Ottawa, and I never had a toothache in me life.

I asked him, "How did you cure it?"

He says, "Down in Gaspe where I live there's no doctors there. There's people that say some prayers or something. They'll come and look at your hand bleeding. I know a man that an axe fell off the barn, and cut his hand like that, and the blood was flying right up – right up in a spout like that – he told me himself. And his people told me. They were putting up a new barn, and he was sitting on a log with his hand like that, and the axe fell off, and struck his hand. So a fellow got on horseback, and went up, and got a fella named Tom Shirley, and he came down on the horse. The fella stayed there, and he jumped on the horse, and come down. And Mr. Whelan told me the minute he looked at his hand the blood stopped. It was coming up like that, spouting up – there was an artery cut or something. It went down and down, and they bound his hand up, and he never had a bit of bother. He never got his hand sewed up nor fixed up nor nothing. They had eight mile to go to the town, and after they bound it up it stopped bleeding, and everything else. Tapp told me that there was no doctors down there, nor nurses, nor no nothing at all except old women, or old men that had a charm, and they'd go to the place, or you'd come to them, and they'd put a hand on your tooth or sore, and whatever it was they done, and you'd be cured.

Now, I went to a son of this old man that cut his hand. I had worked on French River. I'd come down that spring from French River. It was the same year I'd got my tooth cured. A young fella was missing from dinner. So I asked where was Eddy. They said he was lying on the sofa with a toothache. I'd had my tooth cured that spring you see. So I went into the room, and I cured his tooth. He got up off the sofa and followed me out. He says, 'My tooth's not achin' a bit.' I says, 'It won't ache no more.' And that man when he died a couple of years ago had two teeth, but he never had a toothache. He just pulled them out himself when they got loose."

E.F.: Was this Albert Tapp that told you how to do it?

O. J.: Albert Tapp told me how to do it. He had the charm himself from another man, and he gave it to me. I never asked him whether he lost the charm when he gave it to me. I don't know. I can't give it to anybody except another man. If I did it would be no good, I think.

E.F.: Now, if I had a toothache could you cure mine?

O. J.: Yes.

E.F.: What would you do?

O. J.: That's the charm. I can't tell you.

E.F.: Would you do anything while I was here?

O. J.: Well, I would. Sometimes they phone to me, and tell me, and I have little kids going to school come running in with a toothache, and I cure them here, and they go to school, and they never have a toothache. But I can't tell you, you see.

E.F.: But how can you cure my toothache without letting me know what you're saying.

O. J.: I don't let you know. That's the charm, you see.

E.F.: You just say it yourself, do you?

O. J.: Yes, I whisper it meself to meself, and sometimes put my hand on the tooth or something.

E.F.: Well, if I ever get a toothache I'll write to you.

Note: O. J. Abbott's son, Bernard Abbott, says that he thinks his father passed on the charm to him but he didn't pay much attention and, if he had it, he's lost it. He remembers folks coming to the house with toothaches, his father saying something over them, and then they left, supposedly cured.[12]

Books and Recordings by Edith Fowke
at the University of Calgary Library

Books

American Cowboy and Western Pioneer Songs in Canada. 1962. Berkeley: University of California Press.

A Bibliography of Canadian Folklore in English. [Compiled by] with Carol Henderson Carpenter. 1981. Toronto: University of Toronto Press.

Canada's Story in Song. With Alan Mills. 1983. Toronto: Gage.

Canadian Folklore. 1988. Toronto: Oxford University Press.

Explorations in Canadian Folklore. [Compiled by] with Carol Henderson Carpenter. 1985. Toronto: McClelland and Stewart.

A Family Heritage: The Story and Songs of LaRena Clark. With Jay Rahn. 1994. Calgary: University of Calgary Press.

Folk Songs of Canada. With Richard Johnston. 1954. Waterloo, Ontario: Waterloo Music Co.

Folk Songs of Canada II. With Richard Johnston. 1967. Waterloo, Ontario: Waterloo Music Co.

Folk Songs of Canada II. Choral Edition. With Richard Johnston. 1978. Waterloo, Ontario: Waterloo Music Co.

Folk Songs of Quebec. (Chansons de Quebec). With Richard Johnston. 1957. Waterloo, Ontario: Waterloo Music Co.

Folklore of Canada. 1976. Toronto: McClelland and Stewart.

Folktales of French Canada. 1981. Toronto: NC Press.

In Defense of Paul Bunyan. 1975. Bloomington, IN: Folklore Publications Group.

Legends Told in Canada. 1994. Toronto: Royal Ontario Museum.

Lumbering Songs from the Northern Woods. With Norman Cazden. 1985. Toronto: NC Press.

More Folk Songs of Canada. With Richard Johnston. 1967. Waterloo, Ontario: Waterloo Music Co.

Paul Bunyan, Superhero of the Lumberjacks. n.d. With John D. Robins.

The Penguin Book of Canadian Folk Songs. 1973. Harmondsworth, England: Penguin.

The Red River Valley Re-examined. 1964. Berkeley, CA: University of California, 1964.

Red Rover, Red Rover: Children's Games Played in Canada. 1988. Toronto: Doubleday Canada.

Ring Around the Moon. 1977. Englewood Cliffs, NJ: Prentice-Hall. (Paperback edition. 1977. McClelland and Stewart.)

Sally Go Round the Sun. With Keith MacMillan. 1970. Garden City, NY: Doubleday. 1969. McClelland and Stewart.

Sea Songs and Ballads from Nineteenth-Century Nova Scotia: the William H. Smith and Fenwick 1981. Hammer manuscripts. [Edited and annotated by]. New York: Folklorica.

Singing our History: Canada's Story in Song. With Alan Mills 1984. Edition: [Rev. and enl. ed.] Toronto: Doubleday.

Songs and Sayings of an Ulster Childhood. [Edited by]. With Alice Kane. C1983. Toronto: McClelland and Stewart.

Songs of Work and Freedom. With Joe Glazer and Kenneth Bray, 1960. Chicago: Roosevelt University.

Songs of Work and Protest. With Joe Glazer; and Kenneth Bray. repr.1973, c1960. New York: Dover.

Tales Told in Canada. 1986. Toronto: Doubleday.

Toward Socialism. J. S. Woodsworth. [Edited by] 1948 Toronto. Ontario Woodsworth Memorial Foundation.

Traditional Singers and Songs from Ontario. With Peggy Seeger. 1965. Hatboro, PA: Folklore Associates.

Sound Recordings

Authentic Canadian Folk Symbol, English, and American ballads, American Civil War. LaRena LeBarr Clark. Notes by Edith Fowke. n. d. Edith Fowke fonds. Special Collections Accession 416/87.23 file 13.4.

Canadian Folk Sound with LaRena Clark, ballads, Canadian, English, Scottish, and American. LaRena LeBarr Clark. Notes by Edith Fowke. n.d. Edith Fowke fonds. Special Collections Accession 416/87.23 file 13.5.

Canada at the Turn of the Sod, Lumbering, railroading, and sea ballads. LaRena, LeBarr Clark. Notes by Edith Fowke. n.d. Edith Fowke fonds. Special Collections Accession 416/87.23 file 13.6.

Canada's Favourite Folksongs for Kids. Selected by Ralph Cruickshank; notes by Edith Fowke, accompaniments by Howard J. Baer. 1980. Toronto: Berandol Music.

Canada's Traditional Queen of Song, Shanty, Western, Sea, English, Irish, Scottish, Ballads. LaRena Clark. Notes by Edith Fowke. n.d. Edith Fowke fonds. Special Collections Accession No. 416/87.23 file13.2.

Far Canadian Fields, Companion to Penguin Book of Canadian Folk Songs. Notes by Edith Fowke 1974 Edith Fowke fonds. Special Collections Accession 416/87.23 file13.8.

Family Legend in Song, Irish, English, and Scottish Ballads, Lumbering Songs. LaRena Clark. Notes by Edith Fowke n.d. fonds. Special Collections Accession 416/87.23 file 13.3.

Folk Songs of Canada. Sung by Jordan and Sullivan, notes by Edith Fowke. 1954. Waterloo Music.

Folk Songs of Ontario. Recorded by Edith Fowke. 1958. New York. Folkways Records F-4005.

Irish and British Songs from the Ottawa Valley. Sung by O. J. Abbott, notes by Edith Fowke. Folkways Records F-4051.

Lumbering Songs from the Ontario Shanties. Collected by Edith Fowke. Folkways Records F 4052. 1961. Edith Fowke fonds. Special Collections Accession 416/87.23 file 13.15.

Ontario Ballads and Folksongs. Field recording by Edith Fowke. n.d. Edith Fowke fonds. Special Collections Accession 416/87.23 file 13.12.

O, Canada. sung by Alan Mills. Notes by Edith Fowke. Folkways Records FP 3001.

Old Time Couple Dances. Recorded by Edith Fowke. n.d. Edith Fowke fonds. Special Collections Accession 416/87.23 file 13.13.

Sally Go Round the Sun. Collected by Edith Fowke. n.d. Edith Fowke fonds RCA Recording Service. Special Collections Accession 416/87.23 file 13.9.

Songs of the Great Lakes. Collected by Edith Fowke. 1964. Edith Fowke fonds. Special Collections Accession 416/87.23 file 13.14.

The Rambling Irishman. Tom Brandon. Notes by Edith Fowke. 1962 Edith Fowke fonds. Special Collections Accession 416/87.23 file13.11.

Bibliography

Abbott, Bernard. 2002. Interview with Jeanette Panagapka, Ottawa, Ontario.

Atkins Nechka, Ada-Marie. 1998. Edith Fowke: A Celebration. Canadian Folk Music Bulletin 32.2.

Finnigan, Joan. 1975. I Come From the Valley. Toronto: NC Press.

Fowke, Edith. 1965. Traditional Singers and Songs of Ontario. Hatboro, PA: Folklore Associates.

——, and Alan Mills 1965. Canada's Story in Song. Toronto: Gage.

——. The Penguin Book of Canadian Folk Songs. 1973. Harmondsworth, UK: Penguin.

——. Singing Our History. 1984. Toronto: Doubleday.

——. Lumbering Songs from the Northern Woods. 1985. Toronto: NCPress.

——. Fonds, Calgary. Special Collections, MacKimmie Library, University of Calgary. Accession 403/87.10, file 6.2; 416/87.23, file 13.12; 432/88.13, files 1.5, 1.8; 535/93.10, file 4.19; 664/99.21. files 1.39, 2.2, 2.15.

Fowke, Frank. 1996. Interview with Jeanette Panagapka, Toronto, Ontario.

Johnston, Richard. 1996. Interview with Jeanette Panagapka, Calgary, Alberta.

Lavoie, Leo. The Arnprior Story. 1984. Arnprior: H. Brittle Printing Co.

Ross, Val. Lives Lived, Edith Fowke. 1996, 04.08. Toronto: The Globe and Mail.

Discography

Fowke, Edith. Folk Songs of Ontario. NYC. Folkways Records FM 4005 1958.
- Field recordings of the songs of O. J. Abbott. Numbers 1, 2, 3, 4, 5, 6, 13, 14, 15, 16, 17. Collected between 1953 and 1959.
- Irish and British Songs from the Ottawa Valley sung by O. J. Abbott.. NYC. Folkways Records Smithsonian Folkways Recordings 2001 (1961) FM 4051.

Index of Songs

1. Sailor's Bride, The
2. Bold and Undaunted Youth, The
3. Tread on the Tail of Me Coat
4. Erin Go Bragh
5. Johnny Gallagher
6. Chapeau Boys
7. False Young Man, The
8. Near the Shannon Side
9. Young Man Lived in Belfast Town, A
10. Lovely Banks of Boyne, The
11. Keyhole in the Door, The
12. Down by Yon Shady Harbour
13. Dog and His Gun, The
14. Erin's Lovely Home I
15. Erin's Lovely Home II
16. There Was an Old Woman
17. By Borden's Grove
18. Banks of Sweet Dundee, The
19. My Good Looking Man
20. Maid of Sweet Gurteen, The
21. Gypsy Daisy, The
22. Mower, The
23. Farmer's Son and the Shantyboy, The
24. Skibbereen
25. By the Rosy Banks So Green
26. Hat My Father Wore, The
27. Lass of Glenshee, The
28. On the Banks of the Don
29. Lost Jimmy Whelan
30. As I Roved through an Irish Town
31. I'll Write You a Letter
32. Tommy and the Apple
33. Pat O'Donnell
34. Colleen Bawn, The
35. Dying Girl, The
36. Barney Blake
37. My Charming Sally Ann
38. Barley Grain for Me, The
39. Cooper and Donnelly
40. Bunch of Watercresses, The
41. Lonesome Scenes of Winter, The
42. Drunkard's Dream, The
43. Home, Green Erin, O
44. My Bonny Irish Boy
45. Green Linnet, The
46. Daniel O'Connell
47. A Man You Don't Meet Every Day
48. Over the Mountain
49. Blackwater Side, The
50. Banks of the Dee, The
51. Black Bottle, The
52. Terrence's Farewell
53. Old Erin
54. Farmer's Boy, The
55. Captain Goldstein
56. Banks of Newfoundland, The
57. By the Hush, Me Boys
58. Soldier's Farewell, The
59. Bonny Bunch of Rushes Green, The
60. Foggy Dew, The
61. Plains of Waterloo, The
62. Baskatong, The
63. Crúiscín lán, The
64. Golden Vanity, The
65. Finnigan's Wake
66. Kelly the Pirate

Alphabetical Index

47.	A Man You Don't Meet Every Day	60.	Foggy Dew, The
30.	As I Roved through an Irish Town	64.	Golden Vanity, The
56.	Banks of Newfoundland, The	45.	Green Linnet, The
18.	Banks of Sweet Dundee, The	21.	Gypsy Daisy, The
50.	Banks of the Dee, The	26.	Hat My Father Wore, The
38.	Barley Grain for Me, The	43.	Home, Green Erin, O
36.	Barney Blake	31.	I'll Write You a Letter
62.	Baskatong, The	5.	Johnny Gallagher
51.	Black Bottle, The	66.	Kelly the Pirate
49.	Blackwater Side, The	11.	Keyhole in the Door, The
2.	Bold and Undaunted Youth, The	27.	Lass of Glenshee, The
59.	Bonny Bunch of Rushes Green, The	41.	Lonesome Scenes of Winter, The
40.	Bunch of Watercresses, The	29.	Lost Jimmy Whelan
17.	By Borden's Grove	10.	Lovely Banks of Boyne, The
57.	By the Hush, Me Boys	20.	Maid of Sweet Gurteen, The
25.	By the Rosy Banks So Green	22.	Mower, The
55.	Captain Goldstein	44.	My Bonny Irish Boy
6.	Chapeau Boys	37.	My Charming Sally Ann
34.	Colleen Bawn, The	19.	My Good Looking Man
39.	Cooper and Donnelly	8.	Near the Shannon Side
63.	Crúiscín lán, The	53.	Old Erin
46.	Daniel O'Connell	28.	On the Banks of the Don
13.	Dog and His Gun, The	48.	Over the Mountain
12.	Down by Yon Shady Harbour	33.	Pat O'Donnell
42.	Drunkard's Dream, The	61.	Plains of Waterloo, The
35.	Dying Girl, The	1.	Sailor's Bride, The
4.	Erin Go Bragh	24.	Skibbereen
14.	Erin's Lovely Home I	58.	Soldier's Farewell, The
15.	Erin's Lovely Home II	52.	Terrence's Farewell
7.	False Young Man, The	16.	There Was an Old Woman
54.	Farmer's Boy, The	32.	Tommy and the Apple
23.	Farmer's Son and the Shantyboy, The	3.	Tread on the Tail of Me Coat
65.	Finnigan's Wake	9.	Young Man Lived in Belfast Town, A

Index of First Lines

9. A young man lived in Belfast town, courted a girl when she was young
14. As I lay there a-waiting until my trial day
27. As I roved out on a fine summer's morning
61. As I roved out on a fine summer's morning
5. As I roved out on one morning in May
23. As I roved out one evening just as the sun went down
7. As I roved out one May morning
59. As I roved out one May morning to the green fields I took my way
22. As I roved out one morning, all in the month of May
58. As the sun was setting in the west, and filled with evening glee
54. As the sun went down behind a cloud
32. As Tommy was walking one fine summer day
19. Come all you married women and single maidens, too
45. Curiosity bore a young native of Ireland
2. I am a bold and undaunted youth
48. I was always lighthearted and airy, not a care in the world have I
31. I'll write you a letter, it's the last thing I'll send
10. I'm a broken-hearted damsel, I loved a laddie well
6. I'm a jolly good fellow Pat Gregg is my name
26. I'm Paddy Doyle, an Irish lad, I've lately crossed the sea
11. It was on a lovely evening I met a maid so fair
50. It was summer, so softly the breezes were blowing
44. It's once I was courted by a bonny Irish boy
63. Let the farmer praise his grounds as the huntsman does his hounds
36. My name is Barney Blake, I'm a tearing Irish rake
4. My name it is Pat from the shores of Argyle
47. My name it is Pat, I'm proud tho' of that
8. Near the Shannon side there dwelt a lass, a maid both chaste and pure
21. Oh come with me, my pretty fair maid, oh come with me, my honey
24. Oh father, I often hear you talk of Erin's lovely side
57. Oh it's by the hush, me boys, I'm sure that's to hold your noise
3. Oh sure I learned reading and writing
34. Oh the town of Limerick is beautiful, as ev'rybody knows
17. Oh, as I roved out one morning, all in the month of May
30. Oh, as I roved through an Irish town one ev'ning in July
25. Oh, come all you good people, and pray you attend

66.	Oh, come all you jolly seamen, give ear to my song
39.	Oh, come all you true born Irishmen, I hope you will attend
43.	Oh, come all you true born Irishmen, I hope you will attend
42.	Oh, Dermott you look healthy now, your dress more neat and clean
40.	Oh, I am a dairy farmer, from Belveshire I came
62.	Oh, it was in the year eighteen hundred and one
52.	Oh, Kathleen, you're going to leave me
33.	Oh, my name is Pat O'Donnell and I came from Donegal
41.	Oh, the lonesome scenes of winter inclines through frost and snow
13.	Oh, there was a fair lady in London did dwell
38.	Oh, three men went to Deroughhata to sell three loads of rye
37.	Oh, when I was young and boyish my mind was full of glee
56.	Oh, ye may bless your happy lots, all ye who dwell on shore
46.	Oh, you lover's of mirth, I pray pay attention
53.	Old Erin, my country, I love the green bowers
28.	On the banks of the Don there's a dear little spot
51.	One day as I passed through a tavern door
29.	One evening I strayed by the banks of a river
20.	The praises of a lovely girl I mean to you unfold
1.	The sun was setting in the west
64.	There was a gallant ship in the North America
18.	There was a rich merchant's daughter as I am lately told
16.	There was an old woman in our town, in our town did dwell
65.	Tim Finnigan lived on Walker Street, a gentleman Irish mighty odd
60.	When I was a bachelor, airy and young, I followed a raking trade
15.	When I was young and in my prime, my age being twenty-one
55.	You inhabitants of Ireland that's bound to cross the sea
49.	You lover's of this nation, of high and low station
35.	You may raise the window, mother dear, no breeze can harm me now.
12.	You tender hearted lovers, come listen to my grief

Abstract

Songs of the North Woods is a collection of sixty-six songs of one singer, O. J. Abbott (1872–1962), who worked in the lumber camps of Northern Ontario. Collected by Edith Fowke in the 1950s, many of these songs have not been transcribed previously. The songs Abbott sang were ones that were sung by the lumberjacks to entertain each other during the long winter evenings in the north woods. In order to make the songs more accessible to musicologists, performers, and teachers, the transcriptions have been arranged in a musical order from simple to complex, printed by phrase for easy reading and comparative analysis. Charts have been included that analyze each song for metre, toneset, and range.

In addition to the songs, essays provide historical background about Edith Fowke and about O. J. Abbott. Frank Fowke, Edith Fowke's husband, tells, in an interview, about the early collecting trips throughout Ontario on which he accompanied Edith. In another interview, Dr. Richard Johnston, the Canadian composer, reminisces about working with Edith as a co-author and colleague. O. J. Abbott told Edith two stories, which have been transcribed. One recounts the process of cutting square timbers in the logging camps, and the other tells how to cure a toothache by invoking a charm.

Edith Fowke donated her complete collection of books and field recordings to Special Collections, MacKimmie Library, University of Calgary. A listing of the books available through Special Collections is given in the Appendix as well as an index of all of the songs of O. J. Abbott and where they can be found on field tapes, in print, and on recording.

Songs Sung by O. J. Abbott

This list of 120 songs sung by O. J. Abbott is believed to be complete. Songs of the North Woods contains sixty-six songs, all new transcriptions from the original field recordings housed at the University of Calgary. Forty of these have not been previously published. Many of the songs on the Folkways recording Irish and British Songs from the Ottawa Valley sung by O. J. Abbott were published in Traditional Singers and Songs from Ontario, and all but four of these are in Songs of the North Woods. Nine of the songs on the recording are not found in other print sources. Two songs, An Old Man He Courted Me and The Weaver, included below cannot be found on the field recordings at the University of Calgary or on the tapes at the Museum of Civilization. However, they have been attributed to O. J. Abbott in Traditional Singers and Songs of Ontario. It is entirely possible that O. J. Abbott sang songs at later dates that he had not sung for Edith Fowke on her original field recordings. All of the reel-to-reel recordings were assigned an FO, or Fowke Order, number. Late in her life Edith Fowke made a computer listing of all of the songs on her field recordings. It is 237 pages long. In it she lists the singer, the date, the Fowke Order (FO) number, the text of the first line, any published sources, and sometimes a comment (noted below in the right-hand column). It is unfortunate that this valuable list is not as yet on a database. The Museum of Civilization in Ottawa has copies of some of Edith Fowke's collection. Their list attributes thirty-two songs to O. J. Abbott.

The songs and their sources are listed below.

SNW Songs of the North Woods
FO	Fowke Order
MC	Museum of Civilization (tape number)
F4051	Folkways recordings
PBCF	Penguin Book of Canadian Folksongs
LSNW	Lumbering Songs of the Northern Woods
TSSO	Traditional Singers and Songs of Ontario
RING	Ring Around the Moon

Title	SNW	FO	MC	Other	Comments
As I Roved Through an Irish Town	30	1	1		
Banks of Newfoundland, The	56	15		F4051, TSSO, PBCF	
Banks of Sweet Dundee, The	18	1			
Banks of the Dee, The	50	14			
Barley Grain for Me, The	38	13		F4051, TSSO	
Barney Blake	36	13			
Baskatong, The	62	13		F4018, LSNW	
Bellevue Jail		16			popular
Black Bottle, The	51	14			
Blackwater Side, The	49	14			
Bold and Undaunted Youth, The	2	16		F4051, TSSO	
Bonny Bunch of Rushes Green, The	59	1		PBCF	
Bonny Wee Window, The		12, 14	24		
Brooklyn Theatre Fire, The		13			composed
Bunch of Watercresses, A	40	15		F4051	
By Borden's Grove	17	1	1		
By the Hush, Me Boys	57	15		F4051, TSSO, PBCF	
By the Rosy Banks So Green	25	1	1		
Captain Colstein	55	15		F4051, TSSO	
Chapeau Boys	6	13		F4018, LSNW	
Colleen Bawn, The	34	15		F4051	
Cooper and Donnelly	39	13, 16			
Cork Leg, The		16			popular song
Crappy Lie Down		17			Orange ditty
Crúiscín lán, The	63	15		F4051, TSSO	
Daniel O'Connell	46	15		F4051, TSSO	
Dark-Eyed Sailor, The		5	9	TSSO	
Dog and His Gun, The	13	15		F4051	
Doran's Ass		9, 15	18		
Down by Yon Shady Harbour	12	14			
Drunkard's Dream, The	42	13			
Duck Foot Sue		17			
Dying Girl, The	35	16			
Erin Go Bragh	4	9, 15	18		
Erin's Lovely Home I	14	16			
Erin's Lovely Home II	15	16			
False Young Man, The	7	16		F4051, TSSO	
Farmer's Boy, The	54	15			
Farmer's Son and the Shantyboy, The	23	10, 14	19		
Father O'Flynn		14			

Fellow That Looks Like Me, The		14			
Finnigan's Wake	65	9, 16	18		
Foggy Dew, The	60	12, 17	24		incomplete
Foreman Young Monroe, The		14		LSNW	
Gatineau Girls, The		16		LSNW	
Gay Spanish Maid, A		3	6		
Golden Vanity, The	64	2	2	TSSO	
Green Linnet, The	45	1, 13, 16	1	F4051	
Gypsy Daisy, The	21	9, 16	17	F4051, TSSO	
Harry Dunn		2	4	LSNW	
Hat My Father Wore, The	26	16			popular song
Have You Seen Maggie Riley		14			
Heights of Alma, The		1	1	F4051	
Her Bright Smile Haunts Me Still		16			popular song
Hogan's Lake		14		LSNW, PBCF	
Home, Green Erin, O	43	16			
How We Got Up to the Woods Last Year		14, 16		PBCF	
Hughie McCann		17			
I'll Write You a Letter	31	17			
Jack Donahue		5	10		
Jam on Gerry's Rock, The		10	20	F4052, LSNW	
Johnny Gallagher	5	16		TSSO	
Johnny the Sailor		5	9	TSSO	
Kelly the Pirate	66	15		F4051	
Lass of Glenshee, The	27	15		F4051	
Little Brown Jug, The		16			popular song
Little Indian Maid, The		16			composed
Little Old Log Cabin in the Lane, The		17			composed
Lonesome Scenes of Winter, The	41	13			
Lost Jimmy Whelan	29	4	4		
Lovely Banks of Boyne, The	10	1	1		
Maid of Sweet Gurteen, The	20	1	1		
Man You Don't Meet Every Day, A	47	17			
Mary's Ghost		3	6		
Men of Golmoy, The		16			
Mountain Dew, The				F4051	
Mower, The	22	16		TSSO	
My Bonny Irish Boy	44	13		F4051	
My Charming Sally Ann	37	13			
My Good Looking Man	19	16			
Napoleon's Farewell to Paris		1	1		

Near the Shannon Side	8	11		
Nellie Coming Home from the Wake		15		F4051, TSSO, PBCF
No, My Boy, Not I		16		LSNW
Ocean Bee, The		3	6	
Old Erin	53	17		
Old Indian Sat, An		16		fragment
Old Man He Courted Me, An				TSSO
On the Banks of the Don	28	13		F4005
Orangeman's Walk, The		17		composed
Our Ship Was Far, Far from the Land		14		
Over the Mountain	48	16		
Pat McCarthy		13		composed
Pat O'Donnell	33	17		
Plains of Waterloo, The	61	1	1	F4051, TSSO
Pulling Hard against the Storm		13		
Red River Valley, The		13, 17		fragment
Sailor's Bride, The	1	16		
Sally Monroe		5	9	
Ship that Never Returned, The		14		
Silver Herrings		13		F4051
Skibbereen	24	15		F4051, TSSO
Soldier's Farewell, The	58	13		
Terrence's Farewell	52	13		
The Keyhole in the Door	11	14		
There Was an Old Woman	16	13	18	
Three Jolly Jack Tars		5	9	TSSO
Three Men Lay on a Battlefield		13, 14		
Tommy and the Apple	32	16		
Tommy and the Apple		16		
Tread on the Tail of Me Coat	3	16		
Tune the Old Cow Died On, The		15		RING
Twelfth of July, The		17		fragment
Van Diemen's Land		5	10	
Weaver, The				TSSO, PBCF
Wild Colonial Boy, The		5	10	
Yorkshire Bite, The		6	10	
You Are a Little Too Small		16		composed
Young Man Lived in Belfast Town, A	9	13		F4051, TSSO

NOTES

1. The International Folk Music Council (IFMC) was formed in 1947 with the aim of promoting the preservation, practice, study and dissemination of folk music and dance. In 1981 the IFMC changed its name to the International Council for Traditional Music (ICTM), a label that expanded the Eurocentric term "folk music" to include musics of the world. Maude Karples and Dieter Christensen. 2003. International Council for Traditional Music. Grove Music Online. Ed. L. Macey <www.grovemusic.com.ezproxy.lib>
2. Edith Fowke. Letter to Lois Choksy, November 1996.
3. Edith Fowke, with Jay Rahn. A Family Heritage: The Story and Songs of LaRena Clark. 1994. Calgary: University of Calgary Press.
4. Edith Fowke. 1990. Collecting and Studying Canadian Folk Songs. Ethnomusicology in Canada. pp. 295–99 fonds. Special Collections, University of Calgary Library, Accession 664/99.21, file 2.15.
5. This author grew up in a small Scottish, Protestant town in central Ontario in the 1940s with a lively tradition of Scottish folk songs and bagpipe tunes. It's unfortunate that some of the songs from towns like Fergus, Galt (now Cambridge), and Owen Sound, built by Scottish stonemasons, were not more carefully preserved. My childhood repertoire was Scottish folksongs and hymns.
6. Edith Fowke. 1963. Letter to Peggy Seeger, fonds, Special Collections, University of Calgary Library, Accession 664/99.21 file 1.39.
7. Bernard Abbott. 2002. Personal interview. Ottawa, Ontario.
8. Edith Fowke fonds. History of English Ballad Research in Ontario. n.d. Unpublished paper. Special Collections, University of Calgary Library Accession 664/99.21 file 2.15.
9. Edith Fowke collected songs from O. J. Abbott on four occasions: July 31 to August 3, 1957, November 1958, October 1959, and April 1960.
10. Edith Fowke fonds. Irish and British Ballads from the Ottawa Valley, sung by O. J. Abbott. 1961 (FM4051). Folkways Records and Service Corp. New York City, NY, U.S.A. This recording has been rereleased as a CD by Smithsonian Folkways and may be obtained by going to www.folkways.si.edu and searching by artist.
11. Leo Lavoie. 1984. The Arnprior Story. Arnprior, ON: H. Brittle Printing.
12. Bernard Abbott. 2002. Personal interview. Ottawa, Ontario.

www.ingramcontent.com/pod-product-compliance
Lightning Source LLC
Chambersburg PA
CBHW060344010526
44117CB00017B/2961